D0403695

A RECIPE for a MERRY CHRISTMAS

A RECIPE for a MERRY CHRISTMAS

HANDEL H. BROWN
Pastor of the First Presbyterian Church
St. Cloud, Florida

WILLIAM B. EERDMANS PUBLISHING COMPANY
Grand Rapids, Michigan

First printing, October 1960
Printed in the United States of America
Library of Congress Catalog Card Number, 60-53093

FOR DOLLIE,

Wife, lover, companion,
Severest critic, staunchest defender,
inspirer, deflater,
most unpredictable of women,
whom I love more every day.

Contents

One

We, Too, Can Be Wise Men

Did you ever sleep in a bathtub? I am not asking you if you ever dozed off while bathing! I mean: Did you ever line a bathtub with eiderdown quilts, pillows and cushions, and spend a whole long night there?

I remember spending a memorable night like that. Outside it was as cold as the nose of a snowplow. The crisp wind was working overtime to tidy up the whole village and was stretching its long icy fingers to polish the Advent Star.

A rail fence staggered down the steep hill knee high in drifts, and every branch of every tree wore its glistening sleeve of frozen snow. In the misshapen yard far below my tiny window the cars rested under their white meringues, too tired to remove their chains. In the eleventh-century church on top of the hill the bell ringers plied their ancient art more briskly than usual to keep the blood from freezing in their veins.

The house was my grandfather's house, old and inconvenient, with steps in dark corners, where you couldn't see them, which made excellent booby traps for the unwary; and low lintels which greatly amused us small fry, for they never failed to catch some cautious grownup who was watching his feet so carefully that he forgot the dangers to his head!

Grandfather's was the kind of house that catches memories like dust, and that made it particularly suitable as a Christmas rendezvous; and it was there that they wrapped me securely in blankets, and laid me in the bathtub like a mummy in its sarcophagus.

I was too excited to sleep very much, for it was the annual reunion of "the tribes of the dispersion," as we called them, and it brought together my father's ten brothers and sisters with their wives and husbands and children — aunts and uncles and cousins, some of whom we saw only once a year.

They had closed their offices, locked up their homes, and left all their cares and worries behind them to converge upon Grandpa's old, squared-stone house, and infest every corner of it, from attic to cellar.

How could I help but be excited, with holly boughs full of bright red berries behind every picture, over the doors, and in the windows, and with one solitary sprig of mistletoe hidden somewhere in defiance of Grandpa, who considered mistletoe rather risqué!

How could I help but be excited, for there were mysterious whispered conferences which came to an abrupt end if one of us children happened to approach!

It was Christmas Eve, and already the rooms looked rather Christmessy, for you can't let fifty people overrun a house — especially if most of them are children — without having as much confusion as the Old Woman who lived in the shoe.

* * * * * * * * * * *

That's the kind of Christmas we had when I was a boy, and it is only right that I should remember it now, for Christmas is the season of memories, and this Christmas is enriched for all of us by our memories of the long-ago.

Somehow, these precious memories are associated with a special carefree jollity and happiness which were unknown at other times of the year.

From our early-childhood experience we can recall that there was something different in the air at Christmas time . . . something full of romance and mystery and delight . . . something so elfish you have to be a child to feel it – or you must have the childlike spirit.

What is the secret of this Christmas merriment? Why is this abandoned gaiety peculiar to the Advent Season?

The secret of Christmas joy is love and friendliness – a love and a friendliness which are not so obvious at other times and seasons of the year.

We are not always as kind and loving to one another as we should be. We get impatient and short-tempered sometimes, and say unkind things. But as Christmas approaches we begin to change, and we find ourselves thinking kindly of everyone.

We send parcels to our absent loved ones, and we try to choose something that will please them very much. And when we receive their gifts we remark how wonderful it is that they have thought of just what we want to exchange for what we need.

At Christmas we think more highly of our friends than perhaps we do at other times. We appreciate their good points and emphasize them, and we are blind to their faults, for we have eyes of far perspective.

At Christmas we want to forget our quarrels, end our estrangements, and patch up all our broken friendships. We are ready to forgive those who we think have done us wrong, and make a new start on life's path, together.

There was one Christmas when we went to Grandpa's house in a mood of uncertainty. As children, we had been told nothing, but we all knew, or sensed, that there had been a rift in the family during the year. Uncle Fred had offended the rest, some way or other, and no one knew whether he would be there that Christmas.

The greetings were more subdued than usual, and as the groups arrived one after the other, you could see the unspoken question in all their eyes: "Will Fred come?" No! That wasn't it at all. It was: "Will *our* Fred come?"

And then there were only two more cars to arrive — or one, if he wasn't coming — and those two cars were identical: same make, same year, same model, same color. Then one came to the steps at the front door, and there was surreptitious peeping through the venetian blinds. But it was impossible to see who was there, and there was a taut stillness in the room.

Then we heard voices on the porch, and someone opened the door, and there stood Uncle Fred. Suddenly pandemonium broke loose, as if constricting bands had been torn from every breast; and you never saw such hugging or heard such greetings, and no one remembered to close the doors, so that the cold wind blew in on Grandpa, which was unpardonable, and nobody cared, least of all Grandpa, who had momentarily forgotten all about his bronchitis; and Uncle Fred got the greatest welcome of anyone, and everything was all right again.

That belongs to the Christmas spirit, doesn't it? That's how we feel when we enter into the heart of the matter. If we think of the season only as a time for more selfish indulgence, and a vacation from work, then we are false to the whole spirit of the festival. The Christmas feeling is one of friendliness, and it is because we think of others that we are so happy.

This Christmas, let us get rid of all our grudges and grievances, all the unfriendliness, all the hard and uncharitable feelings that poison our systems and that are clogging our minds and hearts. This Advent, let us mean it when we say: "Merry Christmas."

Now it is natural to inquire, Why not be so happy always? If the secret of the joy of Christmas is to be found in kindness and goodwill, why not go on being kindly? Why not continue to cultivate goodwill? Why relapse after Christmas into our usual state of comparative selfishness, with the subsequent usual condition of comparative misery? Why should we entertain the Christmas spirit only for the fugitive moment? Why should not the conversion from selfishness to kindly thought for others be made permanent?

Well, let us remember that the root of this Christmas friendliness is the Christmas *faith,* and you can't have the Christmas spirit without the Christmas faith in the God who revealed Himself in the Babe of Bethlehem.

The angel appeared to the shepherds, saying, "I bring you good tidings of great joy, which shall be to all [the] people"; and these were those good tidings: "Unto you is born this day in the city of David *a Saviour,* which is Christ the Lord."

When we call Him "Saviour," we mean that God has given us everything in Him. He has held nothing back. The utter goodness of God is offered to us in the Babe, for in that Babe God offers us Himself.

It is true that the historic facts of the life of Jesus present us with a personality that is genuinely and undeniably human — the Son of Mary who entered the world as a Babe at Bethlehem. But His impact upon those who knew Him best led each of them, like Thomas, to cry out in adoring confession, "My Lord and my God." In the Babe, God offers us Himself.

But the best gifts challenge our acceptance. A mean heart cannot receive a noble gift. A shriveled spirit cannot receive a generous love. As a big promise demands a big faith, so a large gift requires a large acceptance. God gives out of His infinite resources.

Why do we not continue in the Christmas spirit? Because we do not take what God offers, or, at best, we take only part.

He offers us salvation, and we snatch at safety. He offers us joy, and we greedily grasp at comfort. He holds out love, and we take pleasure. He assures us of eternity, and we want a long life. He gives Himself, and we seize His material blessings.

Gifts challenge our acceptance, and "the unspeakable gift of God" demands for its reception a spiritual desire that is created when God's grace finds a lodging place in our hearts.

God has spoken – have we believed? God has revealed Himself – have we seen? God has given – have we received?

It is God Himself who offers us this joy. I do not understand how anyone can read the New Testament without realizing this, for wherever you open it, you are immediately in an atmosphere of poetry, music, and exuberant joy.

An angel chants to Zacharias the prophecy of John the Baptist's birth. Gabriel's annunciation to Mary is a poem. Elizabeth "cries with a loud shout" when Mary goes to see her, and Mary sings the Magnificat. Zacharias sings the Benedictus when John is born.

The whole universe breaks into music around the shepherds on Christmas Eve, and the shepherds themselves return from the manger glorifying and praising God. Old Simeon takes up the shepherds' song in the Temple and Anna, older still, sings the chorus. Joy spreads like a wave.

The paralyzed man magnifies God for his cure. A rapturous throng glorifies Jesus as He teaches in the synagogue. Praise rises to God as He restores the widow's son at Nain. Wonder and joy are everywhere. His joyous proclamation brings gladness and relief to all kinds of hopeless sufferers.

You see Him, on the eve of His passion, talking about His joy. It was, He said, a characteristic of Himself which He would share with His disciples, "*My joy* I give unto you." It was a gift which no one could take from them, and of which no outward circumstances could rob them. And so it proved to be, for, unless we cannot believe what we read in the Acts of the Apostles, these young and immature Christians, after being imprisoned and beaten, went out *full of joy* that they had been counted worthy to suffer for the sake of their Lord.

Whatever else the Apostolic Church may have been, it was a fellowship of confident and expectant joy. The Early Church counted *joy* as one of the essential marks of the true Christian.

Christianity has often been misrepresented on this point. True, too many factions, squabbles and divisions have marred the Church's history and given some grounds for the story of the six men who were shipwrecked on a desert island. The two Germans immediately got together and organized a society for scientific research. The two Englishmen got together and organized a country club. The two Scotsmen got together and organized the First Presbyterian Church – and the Second Presbyterian Church!

But the Westminster divines of 1643 clearly saw the need to emphasize the joyous aspect of the message of Jesus, and they stressed it at the beginning of *The Shorter Catechism.* The very first question is, "What is the chief end of man?" and those of us who struggled through it will remember that the great answer is, "The chief end of man is to glorify God, and enjoy Him for ever."

What is not so well known, perhaps, is the fact that the Westminster Assembly rejected the first draft of *The Book of Common Prayer* because it was not *joyful* enough, and suggested that "A General Thanksgiving" be included.

The New Testament opens with the angelic choir singing "Glory to God in the highest" for the birth of a Saviour, and it ends with a great company that no man can number singing "a new song" – the Hallelujah Chorus. No wonder it has been called "the most joyful Book in all the world."

And yet, strangely enough, this Christian joy, this Christmas joy, is one of the least acceptable aspects of the Gospel.

People love to dwell sentimentally on the sadness of life, a sadness that is never far away, for just as in God's presence there is fullness of joy, so in His absence there is inevitable sorrow.

There is too much of that dismal cheerfulness that consists of "keeping up our spirits" in "this vale of tears"! Some people's religion seems to say, "Look at me, I'm not complaining, although I have every reason to do so."

So we cherish our sorrows, sorrows from which God, if we allowed Him, would deliver us; and we dwell upon the gloom that we have made for ourselves by shutting out God's light.

Yet "the joy of the Lord" awaits men and women in this day as in the past. It is not a temporary gift. It is not a "shot in the arm" to boost up the drooping spirit for a while. It is not a "tranquilizer" to bring brief respite to the perturbed and anxious soul. It is a permanent and enduring gift. It is a joy which is rooted in the eternities.

The tidings were of great joy because they spoke of a great marvel. They spoke of God stooping down to man, to lift him out of sin and bondage into the glorious liberty of the children of God.

That is still the message, and that is still the condition. Men and women must be willing to put away their evil, and come and worship and adore Him who for their sakes was born and lived and died and rose again, and ever comes to the receptive heart, saying: "These things have I spoken unto you, that my joy might remain in you, and that your joy might be full."

The joy of Christmas is the joy of Christ. It is based on the acceptance of the infinite mercy of God, and it is the joy of those simple souls who have believed to see the goodness of the Lord in the land of the living.

This is the joy of Christmas, and it is the mark of all who have welcomed the Child and entered into the Kingdom of Heaven, because they know that unto them is born a Saviour.

* * * * * * * * * *

Our acceptance of this joy of Christmas is made more difficult by its all-inclusiveness. It "shall be to *all* [the] people."

The gift of God is offered to those who need it, and because it is the gift of grace, it is offered to those who do not deserve it. That is the only way it could be offered to us. Yet just because it is for *all,* it has become a stumbling block to many.

This world loves "exclusives" – fellowships and privileges that are strictly reserved for those who merit them. But the good tidings of great joy are for *all.*

It is this dreadful equality of all in the sight of God that makes the Gospel so unpopular. The Saviour, whose birth we celebrate at Christmas, can be for us only on the condition that He is for everyone. We cannot receive the mercy of God for ourselves unless we receive it also for our neighbors *on exactly the same terms on which it is offered to us.*

Horace Bushnell once said: "Joy is for all men. It does not depend on circumstances, or condition; if it did, it could only be for the few. It is not the fruit of good luck, or of fortune, or even of outward success, which all men cannot have. It is of the soul, or the soul's character; it is the wealth of the soul's own being when it is filled with the Spirit of Jesus, which is the spirit of eternal love."

We must do our part to make this good news known to all mankind. The best way to advertise the joy of Christmas is so to receive the Child into our hearts that the joy of His presence will radiate through our lives. We must let the light of this happiness so shine before men that they may glorify our Father for His matchless kindness and goodwill to all in offering to everyone this same joy.

Christmas, we have said already, is a time of memories. We can, if we like, merely indulge our sentimentality, and worship babyhood and Santa Claus. Or we can let these things be our angels, who come year after year to fill our sky with the vibrant note of joy; and we ourselves can be Wise Men, bringing Him again our gifts.

Our glad hosannas, Prince of Peace,
Thy welcome shall proclaim,
And heaven's eternal arches ring
With Thy beloved name.

—PHILIP DODDRIDGE

Behold, I bring you good
tidings of great joy, which
shall be to all people.
For unto you is born this day
in the city of David a Saviour,
which is Christ the Lord

—LUKE 2:10, 11

Two

The Christmas Road

It is an old road – rough, dangerous, and lonely. From it we can still look down on the ancient town nestling forlornly in a fold of the limestone hills of Judea.

O little town of Bethlehem,
How still we see thee lie!

It was there two thousand years ago, that obscure city, with its unpretentious houses, and its crude inn. Indeed, centuries before that, Samuel anointed David king of Israel at Bethlehem, in the presence of Jesse his father, and his seven older brothers. Before that, it was the setting for the love idyl of Ruth and Boaz; and earlier still Jacob buried his beloved Rachel "in the way to Ephrath, which is Bethlehem."

The site of Bethlehem has never been disputed. From the faintest mists of antiquity it lay much the same, beneath the twinkling stars in the clear Syrian sky, reached by the same rugged road winding over the same steep hill.

There is something very fascinating about a road, especially when it goes wandering over hillsides; for the roads of the world give us a rough outline of the past. Hannibal's fabulous route across the Alps, cut through naked rock and ice, and the ancient roads in the country where I was born contain the very marrow of history.

I know an old Saxon track, a mere fragment, on the open moorland high above the lovely seaside town in northeast England where I lived as a boy. It winds intriguingly across the open country and disappears in the hills.

In contrast to that old, moss-covered lane, and not too far from it, across those same heather-sprinkled Yorkshire Moors, there is a marvelous section of a modern superhighway, wide, and straight as a ruler, where once the Roman legions thundered as they marched to Hadrian's Wall and the chariots of the Imperial Guard flashed by. Sometimes, especially in the delicate morning mist, you can almost see the grey-clad figures marching along in strict military formation, and any time you are in the mood you can *feel* their presence, just as, so they tell me, you can still feel the Redskins when you get on a genuine Indian trail.

So with the rough track that leads to Bethlehem. It rises from the great Roman highway winding in the valleys below.

That highway was the main caravan route from Damascus to Egypt, where, in the spacious harbor of Alexandria, the white-sailed ships lay waiting to carry the commerce of the East across the sparkling waters of the blue Mediterranean.

You can close your eyes and picture that important road, alive with bustle and movement: Roman soldiers in rigid ranks, armored and helmeted, with bright eagle standards glittering above their serried spears; proud horsemen on their prancing Arab stallions; rich merchants accompanied by their fawning slaves; noble ladies in their canopied and cushioned litters, surrounded by their obese eunuchs; rumbling chariots of brass, iron and gilded wood – all the wealth and splendor of civilization poured along that paved highway.

So with the rough track, unpaved, and often muddy, that leads to Bethlehem. It is easy to think of those who once came *that* way, and see them on their journey.

* * * * * * * * * *

First come those two familiar figures with their laden donkey, bought cheap out of their meager savings because it is old and small and thin.

They are plain, hard-working, simple people, content in poverty since they are enriched in soul by the promises made of old to the Children of Israel. They are happy in obscurity, rejoicing in hope, patient in tribulation, continuing instant in prayer, since they know that they – who are of the house and lineage of David – are chosen for a sublime purpose and destined to eternal greatness.

So we see them come, tired and travel-stained, one of them obviously faint and ill, plainly unfit to travel at all. She is no cloistered nun, but a real sister to every woman, and she shares a woman's needs.

When she had listened enrapt as the angel Gabriel made the Annunciation, she had never for one moment dreamed it would be like this. And yet, in the inscrutable wisdom of God, she had been doubly prepared for her divine motherhood – once because she had so little of the world which is seen, once because she had so much of the world which is not seen. Her life was nourished at the springs of faith, and she knew her feet were treading a preappointed path.

At the foot of the hill stands Rachel's tomb, the Taj Mahal of Jewry, that pathetic memorial of a man's great love and a lovely woman's difficult travail and untimely death while on a journey.

This is no place to pause, and with averted head, as if it were some evil omen, she struggles on, turning her thoughts to that far-off kinswoman of her own, Ruth the Moabitess, who, like her, was driven by gross misfortune into the city of David. Would she, like Ruth, find herself the unexpected mother of a race of kings?

Perhaps encouraging herself with such thoughts, she calls to mind the prophecy of Micah:

> *But thou, Bethlehem Ephratah, though thou be little among the thousands of Judah, yet out of thee shall he come forth unto me that is to be the ruler in Israel,*

and bravely turns her attention to the last and steepest climb.

They pause for a moment in the ascent of the hill, for they are almost out of breath, but not quite, and the bearded man repeats a verse from the Psalms in his drawling Galilean speech:

> *I will lift up mine eyes unto the hills,*
> *from whence cometh my help.*

The woman answers in the clearer accent of the Judean folk, finding the simplest words for the sublimest fact:

> *My help cometh from the Lord,*
> *which made heaven and earth.*

It is a well-known scene, and one that has inspired poets of all ages. But good poetry is often sore experience, and so it is on the Christmas Road. There are no angelic wings to bear them up and carry them over the rough places, lest she should dash her foot against a stone. There is no miracle to shorten the weary miles of the long, long way. But they think little of their fatigue, these two travelers, for they belong to another Kingdom.

They regain their breath and, with a sigh – as if for a final effort – they pass out of sight over the crest of the last rugged hill that leads to Bethlehem.

We need not name them. They are history's strangest figures – the carpenter who carved for himself, all unwittingly, so sure a place in the Universal Hall of Fame, and, with him, the mother who mothered more than she knew.

Weary with a journey of more than eighty miles, they find refuge in a cave used as a stable, and there, amid straw and provender and cattle, that night the Saviour of the world is born.

It is a fit birthplace for Him who comes to teach us that the soul of the meanest is as precious as that of the mightiest.

It is a fit birthplace for Him who, in His life of privation, need, and sorrow, has not where to lay His head.

It is a fit birthplace for Him who, from His cross of shame, is destined to rule the regenerate nations.

St. Paul, the very dust of whose writings is gold, has brought the whole matter into proper focus when he says, in Dr. J. B. Phillips' translation:

> *Do you remember the generosity of Jesus Christ, the Lord of us all? He was rich beyond our telling, yet He became poor for your sakes, so that His poverty might make you rich.*

So God in His Son enters upon our human scene, creeping in among us without the slightest disturbance, without a shock to the ordinary framework of affairs, without confusion, jar, or violence.

* * * * * * * * * * *

But soon noise and disturbance are heard along that Christmas Road. The night is hung over with all its stars. The earth stands there in her steady sleep without a sound. The wind has dropped. It is the hour before dawn, and from afar come the strains of strange music. And what music!

> *O never harp nor horn,*
> *Nor aught we blow with breath*
> *or touch with hand,*
> *Was like that music as it came.*
>
> —Source unknown

Yet how well we know it! The glorious proclamation peals forth:

> *Fear not: for, behold, I bring you good tidings of great joy, which shall be to all [the] people. For unto you is born this day in the city of David a Saviour, which is Christ the Lord. And this shall be a sign unto you, Ye shall find the babe wrapped in swaddling clothes, lying in a manger.*

The herald angel's part is done. Suddenly the sky is irradiated with the angelic host. For a brief moment the hillside is alive with their glory.

> *The morning stars sing together,*
> *And all the sons of God shout for joy.*

The heavenly chorus resounds:

> *Glory to God in the highest,*
> *and on earth peace, goodwill toward men.*

When the music ceases, and darkness has fallen once more, we hear rougher voices. There is the stomping tread of the burly shepherds.

We hear them talking, laughing, shouting. We see them, their worn and weary faces sunburnt under their tattered beards; men grown heavy and coarse by their hard life, clad in crude, homemade sheepskin clothes.

We see them strike their crooks deep into the village road as they hurry along the uneven path to Bethlehem. They are filled with excitement, incredulity, hope. Shepherds from the flocks – the ambassadors of the poor.

We can distinguish their animated, expectant cry, "Let us now go even unto Bethlehem, and see this thing which is come to pass." They are going to Bethlehem, not to see *if* this thing has happened, but to see this thing which *has* come to pass.

"And they came with haste, and found . . . the babe lying in a manger." That is all they found. Something so gentle and homey and sweet, this entry of our God. Just a flickering light in a cave under the stars; just a poor hill village, off the beaten path, low and dark amid the huddled stones of the ridge; just the bitter travail and the blessed birth; — just that, and no more. The Christmas Road brought them, in the words of G. K. Chesterton's famous poem:

To an open house in the evening,
To an older place than Eden,
And a taller town than Rome;
To the end of the way
of the wandering star,
To the things that cannot be and are,
To the place where God was homeless
And all men are at home.

* * * * * * * * * *

Some time later, along that same Christmas Road, there comes a group of very different people, richly mounted on camels with tinkling golden bells. We hear the soft dull pad of the beasts' ungainly feet as they come swaying along the track.

Wise Men coming to Jesus. We have made them three in number, and have even invented a moving tale of a fourth who never reached his destination. We have made them kings, and given them names. In Robert Hawker's poem, "The Southern Cross," they become the resurrected sons of Noah:

Pale Japhet bows the knee with gold,
Bright Sem sweet incense brings,
And Cham the myrrh his fingers hold:
Lo! the three Orient kings.

We know so little about them that we picture so much. They are, perhaps, the clearest travelers along that road. We can see them quite plainly.

They are arrayed in dazzling robes, these Wise Men from afar, for they are the ambassadors of the great. They have dark, Eastern faces, these magicians from the mysterious mountains of Persia. They are strong, silent men, with deep-set eyes and curling beards, with rich baggage and many servants. They move with stately dignity.

From time to time their keen eyes search the sky to make sure of their direction – these Wise Men seeking Jesus, who was to be a Light to lighten even Gentiles as well as the Glory of God's people Israel.

* * * * * * * * * *

And then there is another group, different again. They come with angry faces, and the thunder of hasty hoofs, with swords gleaming in the moonlight, spreading fear and horror and suffering and death.

For the traffic of the Christmas Road is not all caravans of peace. Here are the mercenaries of the Edomite Herod, seeking the death of Jesus, hoping to destroy the young Child whom he has feared and hated ever since the Wise Men's tale was confirmed by the chief priests and scribes of the people.

It is a madman's idea to kill all the children to ensure the death of One who threatened to be his rival. It is unspeakably foul and cruel, but the dissolute Herod can brook no rivals. He has already murdered his wife, his mother-in-law, his uncle, and his three sons, Alexander, Aristobolus and Antipater, because he saw in them rivals to his crumbling throne. What is the death of a few score peasant kids to such a monster? His soldiers have their orders. They march over the Christmas Road on their inhuman errand of wanton slaughter of the Innocents.

* * * * * * * * * *

And so we might go on, watching the endless parade along the Christmas Road, calling up strange specters of the past.

Two thousand years have gone, and that road is still there. Perhaps not one of us will ever tread it in the flesh, but if not, in our hearts at least we can walk the Christmas Road.

In the realm of the spirit it is always near, open to each one of us. It beckons us, and the marvel is, it may well be within our own front door, as plain to see as the tinsel twining up the tree, or the paper chains gaily festooning the room.

On the way to Bethlehem you begin to hope and think. Peace and happiness come only when you have ceased to hate and begun to love. Faith in the promises of God helps us to hope in the darkness.

Heaven is not far from the affairs of men, but very near. The heaving of the world's bosom is by the breath of God's Spirit, and all the movements of its ways are in His hands.

Bethlehem calls each one of us to the birth of life's richest Glory and earth's greatest King. It is a journey each one of us can make – if we so desire.

It is so easy to criticize the blindness of the Jews, who misconceived the manner of His coming. Are we among those who have profited by their mistakes? Is the road to Bethlehem, which frightened shepherds once trod, an easy one for frightened modern man to find and, having found, to travel?

The reception of Christ in the human heart is still prevented because of the ox of stubbornness and the ass of doubt. The strange poverty of God's coming repels us still.

Christmas recalls us to the central simplicities. It beckons us to Bethlehem, along the Christmas Road, over the hills of our fears and our troubles, over every barrier and obstacle. It summons us to a journey of faith, which is best accomplished by the simple-hearted.

We can come, running excitedly like the shepherds, pressing on majestically like the Wise Men, or stumbling wearily like Mary or blindly like Joseph. We can come in our need and with our burden, for none was ever more needy and burdened than gentle Mary.

And although the road is lonely and hilly, sometimes deserted, sometimes frightening with its bustling traffic, and at other times spoiled by jarring notes and sinful men, it remains the most desirable road in the whole wide world, for there, if we persevere, our happiest dreams come true because at the end there is the Christ-Child.

On Christmas Eve we make our way to Bethlehem, not to get, but to give; and, coming so, we find ourselves in the presence of God Himself. The Dayspring is at hand, and for all of us it has its message. The Child who is Love Incarnate is there for all who have braved the perils of the road to see. He lies in the manger and if you listen in the stillness you can hear Him say: "You can trust Me. I have come from eternity into time, from heaven itself to Bethlehem, and soon to Calvary, to live and die that you may learn how to live. All that makes life worth living – and possible – I will give you."

"Let *us* now go even unto Bethlehem" and find:

Here is hope, and here is power:
This our world's tremendous hour,
Jesus, Christ of God, descends,
And our night of darkness ends.
(*Source unknown*)

Three

God Made Us To Laugh

The lives of most of us are disorganized around children at Christmas. That is as it should be, for Christmas time is children's time, and Christmas Day is, in a peculiar and wonderful way, children's day. It is the festival of *the* Child, and it is best observed by devoting it to children.

Is there anything more wonderful than a child? Is there anything so unpredictable? so capricious? so exasperating?

Do you ever know just where you stand with your children? Do you ever reach the point where you can confidently foretell what they will do?

It is a very risky business to ask children questions. Sometimes it is positively dangerous. You venture a question, expecting a certain reply, but instead you get something entirely different. Sometimes the answer is so unexpected and so shattering that when you come to yourself in the empty room, you discover your mouth is still open.

It must have been like that with Peter's father. He was a minister, and while he was away at Synod, Peter gave his mother a very rough time. Having a lot more theory than practical, common sense, she could do no more about it than threaten, "Peter, when Daddy returns, I'll tell him everything you've done." And she did.

The preacher was very much upset. He was one of those dignified middle-ageless men who have forgotten that they were ever children.

He shut himself in his study to wrestle with the problem. He regarded it as very serious. It was a challenge to him and to everything he so nobly represented. After mature parsonic reflection, he decided to give Peter a weighty lecture developed on theological lines to a beautifully religious conclusion.

Pompous he might be, but he was wise enough to see that he had to have a cue, so after he had called his son into the study and given him the traditional this-hurts-me-more-than-it-hurts-you routine in the well-modulated tones he usually reserved for Women's Meetings or Lunch with the Bishop, he asked him a predetermined question. "Peter," he said, "why do you think God made you?" Quick as a flash the little fellow, who was a much better theologian than his learned father realized, answered, "God made me to laugh!"

The interview ended immediately, with the usually suave father at a complete loss for words.

* * * * * * * * * *

Does it surprise you to know that young Peter was not original, that he was, in fact, quoting almost word for word from the Bible?

After the birth of Isaac, the child for whom she had long ceased to hope, Sarah said, "God hath made me to laugh, so that all that hear will laugh with me."

May we not transfer these words to the New Testament,

from Sarah at the birth of Isaac to Mary at the birth of Jesus? They suit perfectly the glorious Magnificat:

My soul doth magnify the Lord,
and my spirit hath rejoiced in God
my Saviour.
For he hath regarded the low estate
of his handmaiden:
for, behold, from henceforth all
generations shall call me blessed.

To this great song of rejoicing our Lord's mother might well have added Sarah's conviction about laughter: "God hath made me to laugh, so that all that hear will laugh with me."

It is quite a modern heresy to regard religion as a dismal and gloomy affair, demanding a sour personality encased in a fiercely starched shirt. Alexander Cruden, who compiled the Concordance which bears his name, may be partly responsible. He also published a dictionary, and his definition of "to laugh" was "to be merry in a sinful manner"! But the Master, who had no illusions about life or human nature, often said, "Rejoice," "Be of good cheer."

The Gospels do not portray a dismal or gloomy Christ, nor can we conceive of a melancholy individual receiving the remarkable love which came to Him.

True, in the latter part of His life, as the shadow of the cross inexorably darkened over Him, He seems to have identified Himself with the Suffering Servant of Isaiah. But until "He steadfastly set his face to go to Jerusalem," we find Him a welcome Guest in the homes of the merriest people — boisterous folk from whom the Pharisees turned away in shuddering disgust.

We see children drawn to Him, and we know He watched them playing in the streets, and sometimes their laughing voices and smiling faces were an inspiration and an encouragement to Him.

Would Jesus have been invited to a wedding – the merriest of all Eastern celebrations – if people had regarded Him as a "wet blanket"?

Some of the stories Jesus told are exquisite gems of humor. It is impossible to imagine them coming from set lips and an unsmiling countenance. We can picture Him laughing with His hearers as they appreciated His sallies about the camel trying to squeeze through the eye of a needle, or the man with the trunk of a huge tree sticking out of his eye calmly informing someone that there was a speck of sawdust in his! Jesus loved humor, and in this, too, He was a true Jew.

As Christians we ought to be supremely merry at Christmas, because all our Christmas worship is grounded in the Good News that unto *us* is born a Saviour, Christ the Lord. Dwight L. Moody used to say, "It is the want of Christ which makes men have long faces" – and he was right. John Wesley believed that "sour godliness is the devil's religion," and that Methodists should be a joyous, singing people.

When Christ was born in Bethlehem the Feast of the Returning Sun was given a new and deeper meaning. In the joy of the Christ Mass the merry customs of the old Roman feast were copied but they were hallowed and sanctified. Ancient Rome celebrated the fact that the longest night was passed, and the sun, on its northward journey, promised a rebirth to the trees, the crops and the flowers. The Christian rejoicing was centered in the fact that the Sun of Righteousness had appeared with healing in His wings, to bring to the souls of men, dead in trespasses and sins, a new birth of the Spirit, which made them sons of God and heirs of eternal life. Could they be other than happy?

The New Testament does not promise us freedom from all danger, trial, difficulty, opposition, and worry. Far from it. "In the world ye shall have tribulation" – but it adds immediately, "Be of good cheer"!

St. Paul used the imperative mood when he said, "Rejoice in the Lord always; and again I say, Rejoice!" It is a tremendous word, because it is a word of victory.

It is alleged that the following advertisement actually appeared in a great metropolitan newspaper:

WANTED, LADY'S COMPANION.
MUST BE A CHRISTIAN.
CHEERFUL IF POSSIBLE.

If St. Paul had ever come across anything like that, he would have taken it as a text and preached such a sermon from it that I'm sure there would not have been any young men sleeping in the window seats!

In the primitive superstitions of the dark African jungle, religion does wear a somber shroud. It is a dread burden founded wholly on fear — fear of those evil spirits which are malevolent in purpose, cruel in nature, and arbitrary in punishment.

But the Advent of Jesus Christ, with its joyous proclamation of a loving, forgiving *Father,* makes us sing,

Him serve with mirth,
His praise forth tell;
Come ye before Him and rejoice.

—WILLIAM KETHE

Jesus came to restore the laughter to mankind, to perfect the marred, discordant symphony of happiness, so that all creation may be jubilant in Him.

Happy were those shepherds listening
To the holy angel's word;
Happy they within that stable,
Worshipping their infant Lord.

—GEORGE STRINGER ROWE

It is only when Christianity becomes alive that it really works. Has it lost its influence because we, its exponents, have lost the joy which is the inevitable product of vital spiritual experience?

The dull, though correct, acceptance of a formula has little power to attract attention – still less to win allegiance. Are we failing to win the man in the street because we are not happy enough? You can't sell goods in the market place by showing poor samples. If you don't enjoy your religion – and enjoy it openly and enthusiastically – then, if there is not something wrong with your religion, there is something wrong with you.

There is more harm done to the cause of Christ by unenlightened people who continue a cheerless round of religious observances than by all the atheism and unbelief in the world.

For to continue in religious observances out of fear, or tradition, or habit, or because it satisfies your ego, is to worship an idol of your own making, and that is the road to perdition.

Joylessness in religion is usually accompanied by priggishness, censoriousness, and pride. The long face always seems to go with the long nose – poked into other people's affairs. These, of course, are the peculiar sins of the Pharisee, the one person whom Christ castigated as "a child of hell."

Archbishop James Usher must have had that in mind when he wrote, "If good people would but make their goodness agreeable, and smile instead of frowning in their virtue, how many would they win to the good cause!"

* * * * * * * * * * *

"But," you object, "there isn't a great deal in life to make us laugh. With the world in its present madcap condition, with the rising cost of living, with increasing domestic problems, with terrible crimes reported every day, how can anyone laugh?"

The disruptions of our day bring to mind the old limerick,

God's plan made a hopeful beginning,
But man spoiled his chances by sinning.
We trust that the story
Will end with God's glory,
But at present the other side's winning!

What about *this* Christmas? Is it worth celebrating? Is it right that we should keep it? With half the world behind the Iron Curtain, and the whole world threatened as never before, can we sing,

Peace on earth, goodwill to men?

So far from being an insuperable argument *against* the Christmas festivities, this is one of the greatest arguments *for* them. It is just because the night is so dark that the light needs to shine most brightly. You cannot tell at what hour someone may lose his way in the night because there is no gleam from the window of your soul.

Robert Louis Stevenson believed in his "great task of happiness," and prayed:

If I have moved among my race
And shown no glorious morning face,
Lord, Thy most pointed pleasure take
And stab my spirit broad awake.

We are in great need of such celestial surgery.

Can't keep the Feast because of our depressing circumstances? Then let us read what Dietrich Bonhoeffer wrote to his parents from a Nazi concentration camp:

For a Christian there is nothing peculiarly difficult about Christmas in a prison cell. I dare say it will have more meaning and will be observed with greater sincerity here in this prison than in places where all that survives of the feast is the name. That misery, suffering, poverty, loneliness, helplessness and guilt look very different to the eyes of God from what they do to man, that God should come down to the very place which men usually abhor, that Christ was born in a stable because there was no room for him in the inn – these are things which a prisoner can understand better than anyone else. For him the Christmas story is glad tidings in a very real sense. And that faith gives him a part in the communion of saints, a fellowship transcending the bounds of time and space and reducing the months of confinement here to insignificance.

You see, the truly religious man is always an optimist at heart. He sees God in everything. At Christmas, as at no other time of the year, we proclaim far and wide that at the center of everything there is this one shining fact – God has come to men!

Keep the Feast? Keep it as we have never kept it before! Keep it with our eyes open to its true meaning, to the fact that the Manger holds the Hope of the world. By all means let good Christian men rejoice – so long as they know exactly why they are rejoicing.

There is nothing we should do more willingly, for the Nativity answers so many questions. Indeed, if only we could understand it, we should find that it answers *all* the questions. When the scoffer recites all that's wrong with the world, and then smirkingly asks, "Why doesn't your God *do* something about it?", we can point to the Manger, and ask in reply, "What more could He do than that?" Only those who do not understand the Christmas story, or think the Manger was a failure and the Cross a ghastly mistake, will presume to answer.

We *can* all understand, if only we will keep the Feast with our eyes open to see in Christ the smile upon God's face. Not the amused smile of one who from a distant height looks down for a moment at the futile strivings of us small, human creatures, but a smile of friendliness and understanding.

In Jesus, as St. Paul said, "the kindness of God" has appeared. Here is God coming to share our human problems and concerns with us, making Himself our Brother and our Friend.

When we look on the humanity of Christ there arises, as Martin Luther said, such a light within us that we know what God is: "There is no fear there, but only friendliness and joy."

Now when I say we can *understand* this unique event, I do not mean that we can *explain* it. I mean, rather, that we can not only see its purpose, but *experience* that purpose in our own lives, and that is the best understanding there is. Mentally and intellectually, it is beyond us.

It must be. We must admit that at the center of all our thought about Christmas is a miracle. It is an act of God, whose ways are past finding out. It is a divine event in time, which has meaning for all men and for all time.

But to claim that and not to allow or expect this miraculous happening to make any difference to us would mean that our Christmas celebrations, no matter what we *say,* degenerate into sentimental mythology, and our Christmas rejoicing becomes so much amiable hypocrisy.

It is not enough to keep the Feast with our eyes open, we must keep it with our hearts open too, and perhaps its glory will change us a little, and that will surely make the world a better and happier place for those who have to live with us.

And when we come to the knowledge and understanding that are given to those who keep the Feast with their eyes open, and when we realize the Living Presence of the Living Christ, who comes to those who keep it with their hearts open, we may, perhaps, enter the ranks of the gracious, who not only find joy everywhere but also have the priceless art of leaving it behind them when they go. Their influence is the inevitable gladdening of the heart. It seems as if a shadow of God's own gift has passed upon them. They give light without meaning to shine. These bright hearts have a great work to do for God.

* * * * * * * * * *

Let us make this Christmas "The Festival of the Home." After all, it is children's day, and for their sakes alone we must keep it. Children are happiest when home is important to them, and it will be – if they are important to us.

Don't think of Christmas Eve as "the night before the storm." Relax in the comfortable untidiness of Christmas morning. Find yourself in the elemental reality of giving – just giving.

When your neighbor barges in like a bomber escorted by fighters, remember she *is* your neighbor, and Jesus had something to say even about her. You never know what you may do for her by simply smiling.

It is escapism if you substitute the counterfeit for the genuine, and make your only interest and concern, "How can *I* have a good time?" But if you get into a soul-cleansing understanding of that first Christmas, you will find that it gives you a new outlook on life. You will see the good wherever it is, and encourage it. You will recognize the mean and evil things of life, and find that you have a new strength and courage to fight them to the bitter end.

Keep the Feast. Don't be afraid to laugh. To set a group of people merrily, innocently laughing is to do the will of your Father which is in heaven.

But remember three things. Remember, first, that there are two kinds of laughter. There is the healthy, God-given laugh, which can help and encourage your fellow man, and there is the other sort – the cynical laugh at his expense.

I haven't much use for the man who defines a sense of humor as, "That which makes you laugh at something which, if it happend to you, would make you boiling mad." Such a man does not have a great contribution to make to the well-being of the world. True humor laughs with life, not at it.

Remember, secondly, the words of the Preacher, "To everything there is a season, and a time to every purpose under the heaven. A time to weep, and a time to laugh; a time to mourn, and a time to dance."

There are times when laughter is out of place. I would not preach about laughter on Good Friday, for it would not be merely irreverent, it would be thoroughly blasphemous. Yet it would not be an unseemly subject for Easter Sunday, when the triumphant "Hallelujahs" ring forth. How on earth can anyone say "Hallelujah" without a radiant smile? It is the happiest word in the Hebrew language, and in ours. God will "prove us with mirth" – on occasion.

Finally, remember that when you laugh, you do not laugh alone. "God made me to laugh, *so that all that hear will laugh with me,*" exulted Sarah.

Mirth is more infectious than the measles. See if you can spread laughter this Christmas. Let others catch it from you. Their lives need brightening. Their hearts need cheering. They may be ploughing a lonely furrow. To be lonely at Christmas, to remember its joys as things of the past, to be cut off from family and friends and the goodwill of one's fellows, and only to wish that the day were over – that, surely, is almost beyond bearing. Share your happiness with them. The best part of happiness is the sharing of it with someone else. Many people hold back a smile to see if you have one to trade with them. Have you?

Joy to the world! The Lord is come:
Let earth receive her King;
Let every heart prepare Him room,
And heaven and nature sing.

—Isaac Watts

Four

Is It All a Mockery?

Christmas stands for light in a world of darkness, for truth in a world of lies, for peace in a world of strife, for love in a world of hate, for goodwill in a world of fear. It appears to mock the world because it stands in very sharp contrast to it.

The merriment and the good cheer, the multicolored decorations and the scintillating lights, the pealing bells and the joyful carols, the gaily wrapped packages and the genial greetings – all stand in sharp contrast to normal indifference and unconcern, to the injustice of man thwarting the bounty of God, to the pride of man despising the handiwork of God, to the selfishness of man blind to the goodness of God. The festivity appears to mock the world because it stands in very sharp contrast to it.

But nothing less sharp will do.

Bethlehem is the contradiction of our usual way of life, and of the ever popular doctrines that might is right, every man for himself, and devil take the hindermost.

At Bethlehem we are brought face to face with the things of God. Here, for a moment at least, we can forget the things of men. Here "the people that walked in darkness have seen a great light." That is why we must keep Christmas this year, and keep it with the joy of a basic certainty.

Christmas stands for everything that is opposite to all those things which we fear. It is the flat denial of all those things which must be banished forever if mankind is to survive.

Today the Lake of Gennesaret is troubled by another storm, as Arabs and Jews shoot it out beside the Syrian Sea; yet in Bethlehem lies the secret of abiding peace,

A light to lighten the Gentiles,
and the glory of thy people Israel.

It is because God is there that we are interested in the Babe and His mother, and, even after all the years of disillusionment and frustration, Christmas still has a strange power over the world. It lays its holy touch on even the most superficial. It washes away the years from most of us, and makes us more gay and childlike than we are at other times.

This is because, in our brief pause and change of mood, the beauty of Eternity breaks faintly through the murky smog of Time, and to those who will hush their souls and open their inward eyes, Christmas brings again the great drama of Hope and Love. So "let us go now even unto Bethlehem."

* * * * * * * * * *

For some strange reason we find it easier to understand the Love of the Cross than the Love of the Cradle. Perhaps we have tried harder to understand it. Perhaps we only think we understand it better.

This year, let us try to put ourselves in the shepherds' shoes, and look as they looked, that we may find, as they found, the Hope of the world in a Manger.

His birth was announced by "a multitude of the heavenly host," but it was announced to simple shepherds. They were poor men. Their calling was despised. Their rough homespun clothes stank. They had no great quality – save faithfulness.

It is in the way of duty that heavenly voices are best heard. While the shepherds were doing the mean tasks of earth, there flashed upon them the incomparable glory of heaven. While they watched their flocks by night, the Dayspring from on high illuminated their darkness.

They had no special wisdom that could interpret the mystery, but they might have been asleep! It was a shepherd's watchful eye that first saw the ethereal radiance. It was a shepherd's listening ear that first heard the herald angels sing.

After the angels had gone back into heaven, the shepherds were like little children in the dark alone. It was rather a critical moment when the angels went away, when the divine glory faded, when the revelation from heaven just wasn't there, when they looked into one another's familiar faces, when they peered around them at the common earthly surroundings of land, and rock, and grass, and sheep, when they wondered whether the Divine really had visited them, or whether they had had a strange dream.

Yet these simple men measured up to the test. Hurrying down the hill, and panting up the next, they came, and saw, and were transformed. For them, the whole world was changed.

But the world itself went on utterly unconscious of the coming of God.

They were looking for a king,
To slay their foes, and lift them high;
Thou cam'st a little Baby thing,
That made a woman cry.

—George MacDonald

"The babe . . . lying in a manger." It seems absurd, a cruel mockery of human hope; and so it is, if Messiah's business is to dash the nations in pieces like a potter's vessel.

"The babe . . . lying in a manger." It seems absurd, a cruel mockery of human hope; and so it is, if Messiah's business is to beat down His adversaries before Him, smite them that hate Him, and visit their transgressions with the rod of His fury.

But it is not by might, and it is not by power, that the things of the Spirit win their widening way, but by the changing of men's hearts. And when it comes to changing hearts, "the mailed fist" is not half so effective as the gentle touch of a helpless child – indeed, it is not effective at all.

And because God's thoughts are not our thoughts, because His purpose for the world is not regimentation by force but redemption by love, He sent His Son into the world as a little Child, and the shepherds found "the babe . . . lying in a manger."

Have you ever noticed how, when God does a big thing, He nearly always starts it in a small way?

When the Children of Israel were slaves in Egypt, and they cried to God to deliver them, He heard their cry, and He did deliver them. But He started them on the road to deliverance with a baby – a castaway baby in an ark of bulrushes! And when the time was ripe for the establishment on earth of the Kingdom of Heaven, "God sent forth his Son, born of a woman, born under the law," born in a stable.

Let us look inside that stable, and let us keep on looking during the coming days – let us keep on looking until we are at home there.

* * * * * * * * * *

It had been a hard journey for Mary and Joseph. Their frail donkey had too much of a load for speed. They could not keep up with the other travelers, friends from their own city of Nazareth, and they were alone and weary when, after the sun had set, they laboriously made their way up the winding road to the solitary inn of Bethlehem.

Disappointment awaited them in the city of David. The town was crowded. The inn was full. It was a case of first come first served, and they were the last.

Their need was the greatest. Above everyone else, they needed quiet shelter for *that* night.

It is not difficult to imagine the fruitless anger of Joseph — anger against the pagan Caesar Augustus whose arbitrary decree had made necessary the painful journey, anger against the quisling taxgatherers who ground him down in constant poverty, anger against himself for failing his young wife in the hour of her greatest need. It was a bitter moment for Joseph, and we cannot blame him for his vagrant thoughts.

Yet how much worse was it for Mary! You can picture her, perplexed and wistful, dreaming of her own childhood, as every woman may at such a time.

And what is it to be a child? It is to believe. It is to believe in goodness, beauty, and truth. It is to believe in kindness, love, and friendliness.

What is it to be a child? It is to be a stranger to cynicism, distrust, suspicion, and jealousy. It is to be relaxed and natural, and not stiff with self-importance.

What is it to be a child? It is to be filled with wonder. Life without wonder is hardly worth living. To take everything for granted is to miss the thrill and zest that enrich life and ennoble character.

What is it to be a child? It is to respond openly and joyously to those whose smile bids us welcome to their hearts. It is to accept gladly and thankfully any generous gesture, without imputing unworthy motives and hidden reasons.

What is it to be a child? It is to have faith . . . in faith.

So, perhaps, Mary made the journey back towards her beginning.

That is the way we all must go — Mary, Joseph, or poor shepherd — if we would meet the little Prince who is our Peace. Except ye become as little children, ye shall in no wise enter into Bethlehem's cattle stall.

The trouble with too many of us who talk and write about Christmas is that we aren't poets — and poets are the wisest of our race, for to be a poet you've got to see things other people miss, and you've got to dream dreams and hear voices.

Lord Dunsay once said: "Of all the materials for labour, dreams are the hardest, and the artificer in ideas is the chief of workers, who out of nothing will make a piece of work that may stop a child from crying or lead nations to higher things. For what is it to be a poet? It is to see at a glance the glory of the world, to see beauty in all its forms and manifestations, to feel ugliness like a pain, to resent the wrongs of others as bitterly as one's own, to know mankind as others know single men, to know nature as botanists know a flower, to be thought a fool to hear at moments the clear voice of God."

We have no time to be poets. We are too busy. If we aren't busy finishing something, we are busy hurrying to begin something. "We have no time to stand and stare." We are practical people, set in a practical age, and our whole philosophy is centered in putting our hand to the plow and not looking back, and we have forgotten that Jesus took a relaxed child and put him in the midst and said, "Of such is the kingdom of God."

No hard, embittered spirit can pierce the mystery of Christmas. No Ebenezer Scrooge can find the slightest meaning there. No Mr. Worldly Wiseman can partake of its glory.

For they who to their childhood cling,
And keep their natures fresh as morn,

Once more shall hear the angels sing,
Today the Prince of Peace is born.

—LOWELL

* * * * * * * * * *

The shepherds came in hot haste, their hearts athrob with wonder and expectancy. That is why they, first of all on earth, saw the splendor of God in the stable of Bethlehem. Perhaps they, of all men, could most readily become as little children.

They were filled with astonishment and awe – senses we lose as we grow up – and they trembled on the threshold, not sure what they would find inside. True, the angel had spoken of the Messiah, but in what fearful glory might He be wrapped, this "great David's greater Son"? They didn't know what to expect, and they stood hesitant on the brink of amazing possibilities, and peered into the darkness.

They saw Mary and Joseph – two peasants from the uncouth north come down to pay their taxes – and their hearts sank within their breasts. It seemed a stupid, commonplace sight, no theme for the song of angels. The woman bore little resemblance to Raphael's Madonna, exquisitely robed in cerulean blue. Millet's peasants, toiling in sodden fields under leaden skies, afford a better comparison.

The angels thought more of God's grace to man than man thought of it himself, for it was the *angels* who sang "Glory to God in the highest." The shepherds had no song. They were dumb with disappointment or stupidity.

We stand hesitant today, in this hour of destiny, for we know that we are on the brink of amazing possibilities, and the possibilities for evil seem to outweigh those for good.

We listen in stupefaction as scientists assure us that within the next few years men will visit other planets. We cringe in the shadow of an atomic age, not knowing whether it means atomic bombs or atoms for peace.

We stand hesitant, for we wonder if it is worth our while remembering Christmas as anything but a time to eat, drink, and make merry; and we are tempted to leave all the praise to the angels.

We stand hesitant as we wonder if Christmas *is* only a mockery, for its message of peace and goodwill seems strangely foreign to our turbulent twentieth century.

* * * * * * * * * *

But the shepherds did not hesitate for long. As they gazed into the stable, and their eyes became accustomed to the darkness, they saw, not *two,* but *three,* within that stable. "And they came with haste and found Mary and Joseph, *and the babe lying in a manger.*" That is what the angel had foretold.

No image of God ever made by human hands has really helped the soul in its ceaseless search. No definitions evolved by scholars have ever completely satisfied the active mind about God. No creed has ever been totally free from objection, and no artist's picture has ever been full and perfect.

Since the world began, no one has ever been able to describe the fragrance of the orange blossom in such a way that a man with no sense of smell could understand and enjoy.

No one has ever been able to describe the "Hallelujah Chorus" so as to communicate its unique melodious splendor to someone who can't hear it.

No one has ever been able to describe a sunset so that a blind man could conjure up for himself that glorious riot of color.

Even God could not express Himself finally through *language.* It is too frail and too fragile a medium. It collapses in the hour of crisis.

God revealed Himself through prophet and psalmist, through seer and sage, all through the Old Testament, but a million Old Testaments could not tell us what Jesus tells us. What God could not say by means of a language, He said by means of a *life*:

> *The Word became flesh, and dwelt among us,*
> *(and we beheld his glory,*
> *glory as of the only begotten from the Father),*
> *full of grace and truth.*

The word "religion" has become encrusted with many ideas that are of secondary importance. Mention the word "religion" to a room full of people, and their thoughts fly immediately to the Bible, to the churches they themselves know, to ministers and all the clergy clichés they have ever experienced. Christmas comes to remind us that at the center of Christianity there stands, not a book, or a building, or an organization, but a Person – a Person who sheds light on the purpose of life, on the true value of man, on the sacredness of duty, on human destiny, and on the only way of eternal salvation. He does all this because He is the Word of God to this world.

We do not need to grope our way, "if haply we might find him." We are not left in the darkness to create God in our own image. That was the true Light which came into the world at Bethlehem. The shepherds saw Him, "the light of the world," a tiny, helpless Baby, "all meanly wrapped in swaddling clothes and in a manger laid."

If man had invented this story of Bethlehem we would have had a completely different tale. There would have been no coarse peasants standing in the way, and no needy Child occupying the center of the stage.

We would have had a tall, dark, and handsome prince, strange, strong, miraculous, and alone, except perhaps for the fairy godmother whose magic wand supplied his every wish.

But that is not the way of God. We must see Mary and Joseph first, and then, perhaps, we shall be able to understand the Babe. Without them, the scene bears no relation to us whatever.

If the shepherds had seen a solitary superman, they would have taken to their heels and fled. They saw, first of all, two people *like themselves,* so they lost their fear and began to feel at home. Then, when they looked further and more closely, they found the Child.

Joseph's exterior was mighty rough. His anger vanished into thin air when he saw the Child, but nothing could soften his big, red, calloused hands, and nothing could enrich his common garments. Travel-stained and tired, he looked what he was – a poor, simple, bewildered artisan, completely out of his depth.

But that humble carpenter of Nazareth, that lowly son of the Galilean soil, made the shepherds feel that he belonged to them and, therefore, *the child belonged to them too.*

Christmas, with all its tinsel and trees and toys, with all its singing and celebrating and surfeiting, with all its frolicking and feasting and fun, with all its parties and presents and paraphernalia, with all its cards and cookies and candies – Christmas with all these things is the cruelest of shams and the hollowest of mockeries, unless we know that the Child belongs to us.

I know that most of our busy preparations for Christmas are born of kindness, family affection, hope, and warmheartedness; but a Christmas that is no more than a mid-winter crisis of shopping and cooking is no Christmas.

The Romans observed Saturnalia at the end of December, with the wildest and most boisterous of orgies, during which every moral restraint was thrown to the winds and drunkenness and vice raged supreme. It has been said that the Christian Church took over this celebration and converted it, as it did some others. But Christian experience is very sorrowfully familiar with another fact – that of backsliding – and it is this which seems increasingly to have happened with the observance of Christmas.

But for Christians, its dimensions are too big to make it merely a feast of eating and drinking. Its consequences are too tremendous to pass it off with red ribbon and fancy wrappings.

The Christmas story is neither a pleasant tale nor an imaginary idyl. It is the story of heavenly love in action, of that love taking the initiative and coming voluntarily to lift us up to that fellowship with God for which we were created. This is the message of the New Testament. Christ's birth was no afterthought on God's part. It had been planned before the foundation of the world, and the whole history of the Jews was a preparation for it, without which it could never have happened. It is not only the greatest thing God ever did, it is the pivot on which all His other acts depend and turn.

So imagination and worship must not be suffocated under the mountain of parcels, or even under the Christmas tree.

The Christmas that exhausts us must surrender a little time to the Christmas that exalts us.

The Christmas that is centered in nothing, but is one mad rush over everything, must give place to the Christmas that is centered in the Child, and is a time of rejoicing because He belongs to us.

If this is the reason for all our celebration, if this is the cause of all our rejoicing, if this is the center of all our hope, if the knowledge that *the Child belongs to us* is at the root of all our merriment, then Christmas is not a mockery; it is the most relevant, practical, and powerful thing in our lives, and we have got to publish far and wide the glad tidings,

"The Child belongs to us!"

We, the sons of men, rejoice,
The Prince of Peace proclaim;
With heaven's host lift up our voice,

And shout Immanuel's name;
Knees and hearts to Him we bow,
Of our flesh and of our bone,
Jesus is our Brother now,
And God is all our own.

—CHARLES WESLEY

Five

The Meaning of Christmas

When Matthew quoted the glorious prophecy of Isaiah, "Behold, a virgin shall conceive and bear a son, and they shall call his name Immanuel," he was inspired to add a simple explanation, "which being interpreted is, God with us" — and I, for one, am very thankful for that interpretation.

We need it. If Matthew had left it out, I'm sure some enlightened copyist, laboriously writing the text with loving care, would have put it in.

Without it there would merely be the prosaic information, "They shall call his name Immanuel," which wouldn't mean very much more to us than, "They shall call his name William."

But the explanation *is* there: "Immanuel, which being interpreted is, God with us"; and the page lights up like some dull morning in November when the sun suddenly and unexpectedly explodes in the eastern sky, transforming it into June, warm with love, vibrant with meaning, fragrant with hope.

"Immanuel . . . God with us." It is the authentic speech of the still small voice. It comes as a whisper, soft as the glow of altar candles, too low to awaken the Babe sleeping in the manger.

Bishop Phillips Brooks caught the spirit of it when he wrote,

How silently, how silently,
The wondrous gift is given.

Quiet as a sunbeam climbing a tree on the heels of a cloud, it banishes the drabness of winter as the windows of our hearts become gold-plated with the sunshine of God's love,

So God imparts to human hearts
The blessings of His heaven.

So God imparts the supreme blessing, which we call "Immanuel," and we rejoice with exceeding great joy because it means "God with us."

* * * * * * * * * *

In a sense, "God with us" is not a new message. What is new is the language in which it is spoken. But it is a mistake to think that the world was without God until Jesus was born.

We see God in creation, making something for Himself, and putting Himself into that something which He made.

We understand the doctrine of Providence to mean that God has always been so concerned for His people that He has never left them wholly to their own devices, but has overshadowed them with His presence, even when they knew it not.

There are great movements in the story of our race which suggest that while history must not be interpreted in any mechanical way, yet there is such a pattern in it that we can tell the direction in which it is moving, and discern the presence of the Prime Mover, who is guiding it to the end which He Himself has chosen.

We know from our own lives – from what we call "conscience" – that we are different from the birds of the air and the beasts of the field.

We know, perhaps from *remorse* more clearly than from any other source, that we are called to walk an ascending path, although we are perfectly free to ignore the call.

The Old Testament says, "He made known his ways unto Moses, his acts unto the children of Israel," and we accept that statement as true. It is forced upon us by the sheer weight of the evidence. The more we know of the other nations of antiquity, the more marvelous does the Jewish nation appear. We are left with no explanation other than this: "God, at sundry times and in divers manners, spake in time past unto the fathers in the prophets."

If we look a little more closely at the Old Testament, we shall find that the basic idea contained in "Immanuel" is not unknown to the writers of the sacred books. "God with us" is something they earnestly believed. Listen to them:

"Certainly I will be with thee."
"The Lord thy God is with thee
withersoever thou goest."
"My presence shall go with thee."
"Cast me not away from thy presence."
"In thy presence is fulness of joy."

Yet all this is inadequate and insufficient. There is something lacking. God in Creation, God in Providence, God in History, God in Conscience, God in the Old Testament – all this leaves us needy and unsatisfied.

We see Him dimly and indistinctly. We know there's *something* there, but we are not sure what. It's like a man half-blind with cataracts peering into a mirror half-blind with age.

With nothing more we would ever cry, "My soul thirsteth for God, for the living God. . . . O that I knew where I might find him!" And our faith would be reduced to that of the Indiana farmer who, commenting on his poor harvest, said, "My wheat didn't do as good as I thought it would – but then, I never thought it would"!

The Old Testament is the *Bible* of the Jew. It closes with the Book of Malachi, which means, for the Jew, that the revelation of God ends there too. But the Jew is not content. The Patriarchs and Prophets of Israel confess longings too deep to be satisfied with anything they have received. They acknowledge the incompleteness of what they have. Their greatest desire is to be able to say with utter finality and assurance, "God with us."

* * * * * * * * * *

Our Bible does not end with Malachi. Indeed the vital *Christian* message does not begin until we come to Bethlehem, to "a lowly cattle stall," and we chant in adoration,

Glory be to God on high,
And peace on earth descend:
God comes down, He bows the sky,
And shows Himself our Friend!
—CHARLES WESLEY

"Immanuel – God with us."

"God hath spoken unto us – in a Son."

The stupendous thing to which the writers of the Old Testament constantly refer is the deliverance of the Children of Israel from the bondage of Egypt – that amazing manifestation of unparalleled might by which the first-born of the land were cut off, the impoverished slaves loaded with riches and jewels, the inanimate Red Sea made to obey the command of the Most High, the pride of Pharaoh's army destroyed, and the Children of the Covenant brought to safety and freedom.

But the great thing to which *we* look back is the birth of a weak and helpless Baby in all the poverty, filth and stench of an Eastern stable.

Haste with the shepherds, see
The mystery of grace;
A manger bed, a Child,
Is all the eye can trace.

—CHARLES COFFIN

And "mystery of grace" it is. The mystery of it increases the more we

keep and ponder in our mind,
God's wondrous love in saving lost mankind.

—JOHN BYROM

A key is needed to open that mystery, and yet I am afraid that the lock is on our own minds. We still try to measure God by the yardstick of our "common sense," thinking the things of men instead of the things of God.

God always surprises us. His ways are not our ways. Can you imagine a more unlikely way for the Son of God, the Saviour of the world, to come to earth than the way He did come? It shows how little God thinks of our nice distinctions, of our ideas of what is becoming, proper, and fitting. We say: "The best for the best, and the poorest for the poorest." God works in exactly the opposite way: "The things that are despised hath God chosen."

Christmas, if it means anything at all, means the consecration of the commonplace. For what could be more common than a cradle, or more ordinary than a baby? Almost every house has a cradle, or has had one in its history. And in its appropriate time it has been the meeting point of the commonplace things of home and family life: washing, feeding, crying, laughing, waking, sleeping, playing, learning, growing, grumbling — all those human activities which are so common that we live through them and with them without thinking. Christmas is a continual reminder that God in Christ has consecrated the commonplace things of life to confound those that are mighty.

There is no human standard by which the importance

of Bethlehem can be reckoned. Bethlehem is itself the standard by which the importance of all human activity must be judged; but Bethlehem, like the Cross, is "unto them that are perishing, foolishness."

"Like the Cross" . . . perhaps in that comparison we have a clue to the meaning of Christmas, for it *is* "like the Cross."

The whole life of Jesus, from beginning to end, is of a piece. It is a seamless robe. No part of it, whether it is the beginning or the end, is understood properly until it is understood in the light of the whole, and as part of the whole.

Bethlehem is a parable of the whole life of Jesus. He was born an outcast, in a rough stable, with the winds of God beating upon Him. For years He earned a livelihood for Himself, and for the rest of the humble family to which He belonged, by the taut muscles and calloused hands of a manual worker.

The day came when He, whose dwelling had been heaven, had nowhere to lay His head. A certain village once refused Him a night's lodging. "He came unto his own, and his own received him not."

He was despised and rejected of men, a Man of Sorrows and acquainted with grief. He died an outcast, crucified on a hill outside the city wall, with the winds of God beating upon Him.

Everything in the life of Jesus fits into one great design – the Cradle and the Cross, the Manger and the Ministry. All the many parts of His life tell us that He came for one purpose, and that in everything His purpose was one. He was rich, yet for our sakes He became poor, that we, through His poverty, might become rich.

From the Manger to the Cross, through all the tortuous wanderings and fluctuating fortunes of that unique life, in all He ever was, more than in all He ever said, there is one amazing message.

It is there as He stands before His frenzied parents in the Temple when He was twelve years old. It is there as He places a meek child in the center of the squabbling, jealous disciples. It is there as He feels in an empty pocket for tax money.

It is there as He weeps over Jerusalem. It is there as He rides a borrowed donkey for His Triumphal Entry. It is there as He calmly tells a perplexed Roman governor that the power he thinks comes from Caesar actually comes from God.

It is there as, in the agony of His death, He cries, "Father, forgive them, for they know not what they do." It is there "from the poor manger to the bitter Cross." It is there, in Bethlehem, in that crude stable where

Cold on His cradle the dew-drops are shining;
Low lies His head with the beasts of the stall.

—REGINALD HEBER

What is there?

Is this the Eternal Son
Who on the starry throne
Before the worlds begun
Was with the Father one?

—CHARLES COFFIN

* * * * * * * * * *

Having eyes we see not, and having ears we hear not.

We come, year after year, to Bethlehem, and whether we are Wise Men, which is very unlikely, or whether we are simple shepherds, which is far more likely, we kneel by the manger. *But what have we learned from our annual pilgrimages?*

We come, year after year, to Calvary. Through the forty days of Lent we follow the wandering steps of the Master as they lead to Bethany, to Jerusalem, to the Garden of Gethsemane, to Pilate's Judgment Hall, to Golgotha. We see Him condemned, scourged, crucified. *But what have we learned from our annual vigils?*

Have we ever tried to relate Christmas to Good Friday? Do we realize that they have the same common denominator, that, in each case, the answer is the same?

Too many of us have minds like concrete — made up of innumerable fragments, all mixed up, and permanently set.

We sentimentally sing,

Away in a manger, no crib for a bed,
The little Lord Jesus laid down His sweet head.
The stars in the bright sky
Looked down where He lay,
The little Lord Jesus asleep on the hay.

—MARTIN LUTHER

But what does it mean?

What is there?

The way He entered this world which He had made, and the way He left this world which had no room for Him, and the whole pattern of His life reveal: glory in humiliation, sovereignty through suffering, perfection through limitation, victory through defeat, Godhead inherent in manhood, "Immanuel — God with us."

Yes, faith can pierce the cloud
Which shrouds His glory now,
And hail Him God and Lord,
To whom all creatures bow.

—CHARLES COFFIN

All praise to Thee, Eternal Lord,
Clothed in a garb of flesh and blood;
Choosing a manger for Thy throne,
While worlds on worlds are Thine alone.

—MARTIN LUTHER

When we accept this great fact itself, we may well ask ourselves, "Why should this incredible thing happen?" The first and most important part of the answer was given by St. Augustine: "The chief cause of Christ's coming was that men might know how much God loves them." In the presence of the Babe, argument ends in adoration, the rich fall down in homage, and the poor stand up in hope.

The second and subsidiary part of the answer has already been given — to consecrate the commonplace. The consecration of the commonplace is the dynamic nerve-center of the Christian faith. For it was by His incarnate human life that the Lord Jesus made common things important and glorious.

That is why the Gospels are central to the Christian way of life, for they tell us all that we know of God's gracious acts in a human context.

Christmas is a reminder to us that when we take the mystery out of Christianity we are left with a moralistic sect, of no relevance to life save only to the eccentric, for it is the divine humanity of our Lord which turns the "Tears of Things" into the tears of Christ Himself.

"Choosing a manger for Thy throne"! "For God so loved the world, that he gave his only begotten Son." He gave because He loved. It is the way of love to give, and the measure of the love is the measure of the sacrifice involved in the gift.

* * * * * * * * * *

Christmas is traditionally the season of giving, and because it is the season of giving, it must be, also, the season of receiving.

We keep our parcels and presents for Christmas Day. They may have arrived weeks before, from who knows where, beribboned reminders of the affections of those we love. But we do not open them the minute we get them.

One of the characteristics of the Christmas pilgrimage is its element of surprise. To the youngest it brings the unveiling of "great secrets." Half the joy of Christmas morning comes from the surprises we receive, whatever our age, as we feverishly tear off the gay wrappings. The squeals of delight that echo and re-echo from the children, as their eyes stand out like lollipops, are indications of pleasure at the gifts they receive, of course, but they are quite as much exclamations of surprise, that surprise which furnishes half the pleasure.

There is no surprise more magical than the surprise of being loved. It is the finger of God on our shoulders. On Christmas Day, He lays His whole hand upon us, for as we gaze at the lowliness of the Manger, seeing glory in humiliation and realizing something of the sacrifice involved, He says to us again, "I love *you,* like that." "God so loved the world, that he gave – his only begotten Son."

Our loved ones may be far away. We may not be able to see them, although we long to do so. They send us their Christmas greetings, and, sometimes, they send the best greeting of all, "We are coming to spend Christmas with you," and we are thrilled at just the thought of their company.

God has sent us His message, which we call "Immanuel," and we rejoice that it says, "God with us"; and as we look again at that stable, seeing glory in humiliation, we know He *is* with us, and we rejoice in

God's presence and His very self,
An essence all-divine.

—JOHN HENRY NEWMAN

O Child! Thy silence speaks,
And bids us not refuse
To bear what flesh would shun,
To spurn what flesh would choose.
Fill us with holy love,
Heal Thou our earthly pride;
Born in each lowly heart,
For ever there abide.

—CHARLES COFFIN

Six

Peace on Earth — What Is It?

We are all acquainted with some unfortunate individuals who suffer from chronic "sneersightedness." The less intelligent they are, the more they are scornful; and the less they know about life, the more blasé they are.

The angelic declaration, "On earth peace," is a word at which they really sneer. "Where?" they ask – and perhaps you have trouble in answering.

In individual, national, and international affairs, it seems to be the same story. You can hardly read any newspaper without getting the impression that mankind is about as peaceful as a bunch of wildcats tied tail to tail and thrown into a sack.

When you turn from a consideration of domestic life to a perusal of the world situation, the picture is even more depressing. "On earth peace" – where?

Between pro-French and pro-Nationalists in Algeria? Between Chinese Nationalists and Chinese Communists? Between Muslims and Hindus in India? Between Jews and

Arabs in Palestine? Between employers, employees, and various governmental agencies in this country? Between Soviet Russia and her satellites on the one hand, and the outside world on the other? "On earth peace"?

No. Rather: hatred, jealousy, fear and distrust, which embitter life, destroy its most sacred relationships, devastate homes, break up communities, and lead ultimately to wars with millions of young men slain, women's hearts broken, children starved, and minds rendered insane.

"On earth peace." "Where," asks the cynic, "in history?" No, this angelic declaration has been denied and falsified by every one of the so-called "Christian" centuries, as surely as it is mocked by the carnage of our time. Perhaps a better text would be, "I came not to bring peace, but a sword."

Unfortunately — or is it *fortunately?* — the matter is not quite so simple as that. The angelic declaration, "On earth peace," stands at the very heart of the Christmas story, and is essential to the proclamation of the Christian gospel. It must mean *something*. The question is, What?

* * * * * * * * * *

Perhaps the first thing we ought to realize is this: *these words were spoken in a world that already had peace.*

In ancient Rome there was a shrine dedicated to the god Janus. Whenever the Romans went to war, the doors of that shrine were opened, so that Janus could go with them and bring them victory.

For two hundred years those doors had never been closed. First there was the war against Carthage, then the great imperialistic wars against Macedon and Syria, and finally two generations of civil war within the empire itself.

But when Augustus emerged as the victorious Caesar, he brought peace to a weary world — the long enduring *Pax Romana.* The doors of the shrine of Janus creaked back upon their rusty hinges, and that night when the angels sang at Bethlehem, peace reigned over the civilized world.

In 1645, young John Milton published his *Ode to the Nativity,* the most exquisite piece of word music that has ever been composed in the English language. In it he reminds us of the peace that was on earth the night Jesus was born.

But He, her fears to cease,
Sent down the meek-eyed Peace;
She, crown'd with olive green, came softly sliding
Down through the turning sphere,
His ready harbinger,
With turtle wing the amorous clouds dividing,
And waving wide her myrtle wand,
She strikes a universal peace through sea and land.

No war, or battle's sound
Was heard the world around:
The idle spear and shield were high uphung;
The hookèd chariot stood
Unstain'd with hostile blood,
The trumpet spake not to the armèd throng
And kings sat still with awful eye,
As if they surely knew their sovran Lord was by.

But peaceful was the night
Wherein the Prince of Light
His reign of peace upon the earth began:
The winds, with wonder whist,
Smoothly the waters kist,
Whispering new joys to the mild ocean –
Who now hath quite forgot to rave,
While birds of calm sit brooding on the charmèd wave.

"On earth peace." To us the angels seem to have been two thousand years too early, but to Caesar Augustus they would have seemed twenty years too late. How could God give them something that was already theirs?

There can be only one answer to that question. Peace meant one thing to Augustus, and quite another thing to God. But, lest we be hasty in our condemnation of the emperor, let us ask ourselves just what "peace" means to us.

There are so many varied conceptions of peace that it would take a special study adequately to describe and analyze them. And yet if they are classified, it seems to me that they fall into four major groups or types, which may briefly be mentioned here.

There is that kind of peace which is the hope and desire of the very old and the very tired. Their race is run. They are completely exhausted. Their strength has turned to weakness. For them, peace is absolute tranquillity, with no movement on the waters of life, no ripple, no ebb and flow, no rising and falling, but only stillness and quietness, "as though to breathe were life." It is the peace of approaching death, and its end is stagnation.

Many people live on the animal level, and their idea of peace reflects this. For them, peace is the enjoyment of physical ease and comfort, summed up in the famous phrase, "a full belly and a good bed." Peace, for them, is the absence of hardship and calamity, worry and trial. What they do not realize is that tribulation does not destroy peace, but the resistance of our stubborn wills to such experiences and our refusal to be in harmony with the eternal purpose, and say "Thy will be done," cause heartache and unease.

There is probably nothing more pathetic than a weak and harassed mother, exhausted by much childbearing, and worn out by the constant fight to keep the wolf from the door. She has taken so much that she can take no more. Anything is better than this continual struggle. She must have peace, *at any price.* She is willing to give in every time, if only the children will keep quiet and let her have a little peace. We have seen the same attitude in international affairs. But if contemporary history teaches us anything at all, it is that *appeasement* is a dirty word.

Then there is the conception of peace that is often associated with humanism, and that finds classical expression in Tennyson's famous poem, "The Parliament of Man."

For I dipped into the future,
far as human eye could see,
Saw the vision of the world,
and all the wonder that could be;
Saw the heavens fill with commerce —
argosies of magic sails,
Pilots of the purple twilight
dropping down with costly bales;
Heard the heavens fill with shouting,
and there rained a ghastly dew
From the nations' airy navies
grappling in the central blue.
Far along the worldwide whisper
of the southwind rushing warm
With the standards of the people
plunging through the thunderstorm,
Till the war drums throbbed no longer
and the battle flags were furled
In the Parliament of Man,
the Federation of the World.

Tennyson spoke prophetically when he described "the nations' airy navies grappling in the central blue." All this has happened, but the battle flags are not yet furled. We have the Parliament of Man in the United Nations, and we are thankful for it. We have all the machinery for peace, and would be much worse off without it, but we live constantly in a state of cold war that, at any moment, might flare up into an ugly universal conflagration. Man has the *means* of peace, but what the humanist forgets is that he lacks both the *will* and the *power*.

To the Roman emperor, peace meant the absence of war. To us, peace means so many things that we don't know what it means. To God, peace means the presence of a new kind of spirit. It is not through change of circumstances that God gives peace, but through change of character.

Augustus was a brilliant statesman as well as a great warrior, but what he understood by peace is not the divine understanding, any more than ours is. There is an older strife than the war of man with man,

> *Hear, O ye mountains, the Lord's controversy,*
> *and ye enduring foundations of the earth;*
> *for the Lord hath a controversy with his people.*

Before man ever made man his enemy, he made God his Adversary. This is his supreme tragedy, greater by far than any war, however global and ghastly.

The fundamental failure of human history is not that man cannot live at peace with man his brother; it is that he will not live at peace with God his Father.

The Bible says that man is the child of God. At the heart of the whole Christian revelation is the central and unique teaching of Jesus that God is *Father.*

But the Bible nowhere ministers to human pride. It says that although man is a son of God, he is a prodigal son. It says that he is willful, proud, selfish, and desperately wicked, *because he has rebelled against his Father.*

It is the Fatherhood of God that makes human sin so utterly terrible and depraved. Sin against a king, or ruler, is rebellion against impersonal, external authority; but rebellion against a *Father* is spitting in the face of love. The former breaks a law. The latter breaks a heart.

The Fatherhood of God says that we are not earth-born, but God-born, that we are winged souls fitted to cleave the air in upward flight, thrilling the firmaments with the music of our praise, and heaping love upon the Source of all love.

We are very conscious that we are not what we ought to be, that we are not what we were made to be. We have rebelled against our Father, and the result is all the ills that flesh is heir to, all the confusion and perplexity of loneliness, all our lostness, all our bewildered sense of bewilderment, all our nostalgic sense of belonging and yet not knowing where we belong. The result is that we are at war with ourselves, our neighbors, our world, and our daily lot – all because we are not at peace with God.

The most tragic fact in the universe is that He who is the Lord God Omnipotent should know

How sharper than a serpent's tooth it is
To have a thankless child.

—SHAKESPEARE (King Lear)

It fills creation with amazement:

Hear, O heaven, and give ear, O earth!
I have nourished and brought up children
and they *have rebelled against me.*

The fundamental failure of human history is not that man cannot live at peace with man his brother; it is that man will not live at peace with God his Father.

If we believe this, then "on earth peace" will mean something to us.

* * * * * * * * * *

One of the carols which is often sung during the Advent season says,

For lo! the days are hastening on
By prophet bards foretold,
When with the ever-circling years
Comes round the age of gold.
When peace shall over all the earth
Its ancient splendors fling,
And the whole world give back the song
Which now the angels sing.

—EDMUND H. SEARS

But it is simply not true. This is not the message of the New Testament. This is the hope of Greek philosophy.

When Jesus met His disciples after the Resurrection, the first word He spoke to them was "Peace." His final word before He left them was, "My peace I leave with you." This was something they expected, because all through His earthly ministry He had forgiven sinners with the words, "Go in peace."

In the Second Epistle to the Thessalonians, Jesus is called "the Lord of peace." God is called "the God of peace" five times in the Epistles. St. Paul's prayer for the Philippians was that "the peace of God which passeth all understanding" should be their safety and protection. *This peace was not a future ideal, it was a present experience.*

"On earth peace." We shall find a clue to the meaning of these words if we consider the time when they were first uttered.

The angelic declaration was made on Christmas Eve. The first faint cry in the stable had hardly been heard. Neither Wise Men nor shepherds had seen Him. Indeed no eye had looked upon Him save the eyes of Mary and Joseph. No word of grace had been spoken. No deed of power was, as yet, accomplished. Nothing – but His Presence. *That very Presence is the Peace of God.*

You cannot separate Christ's gifts from Christ. The only way to get anything He gives is to get Him. It is His holy Presence that does everything. "With Christ in the vessel, I smile at the storm."

Janus returned to his Roman shrine, and nothing was changed. The Eternal Son came forth from the bosom of the Father, and was found in manhood of the blessed virgin Mary, and everything was changed.

This angelic declaration takes us to the very heart of Christianity. "He is our peace," not by what He *does,* but by what He *is.*

Our God contracted to a span,
Incomprehensibly made man.
—CHARLES WESLEY

God has visited and redeemed His people. This world is no abandoned or blighted planet in a limitless void of sky. We have not been forsaken. God has come. God Himself is with us. He has pledged Himself in love to this world. Nothing can ever be the same again.

The soft light from a stable door
Streams o'er the world of men,
Whatever clouds may veil the sun,
Never is night again.
(*Source unknown*)

At Bethlehem we see the infusion of humanity with divinity, and in that great act is our peace. The climax of the human drama is not

The one far-off divine event
To which the whole creation moves;

it has been reached already — in a stable!

A few years ago, a five-year-old little girl, whose parents often went out for the evening, was rehearsing at home for the children's Christmas service. I don't know whether the mother thought it was time she spent more evenings with her daughter, but she was certainly surprised to hear her sing,

Hark! the herald angels sing
Glory to the newborn King!
Peace on earth and mercy mild,
God and sitters *reconciled!*

That may be a sign of the times!

The correct version of that stanza *is* the message of the New Testament. "Peace on earth and mercy mild" depends on "God and sinners reconciled." Wherever sinners are reconciled to God through His Son, there *is* "peace on earth."

Wherever men receive Jesus as their Saviour, the miracle of Bethlehem is repeated. Christ is born anew in the hearts of His humble followers, and the divine is once more realized in the human. *That* is "peace" – "the peace of God which passeth all understanding."

Only as God is at the center of the world as Lord of all life can there be any peace among men, for peace is a state of heart and mind arising out of a right relationship with God.

In the world of everyday living, this does not always bring tranquillity; comfort cannot always be associated with it; it never involves appeasement; it always demands obedience. Obedience is peace, and in His service is perfect freedom.

We cannot come into the presence of Perfect Goodness without feeling its moral challenge. We cannot recognize that Christ is near us without hearing Him say, "Follow me." It is in accepting the moral challenge and being obedient to the call that true peace is found.

* * * * * * * * * *

"On earth peace" is not the whole story. It is only part of the angelic declaration. The heavenly choir sang the Gloria in Excelsis:

> *Glory to God in the highest,*
> *and on earth peace among men*
> *in whom he is well-pleased.*

We pick out "on earth peace" because that appeals to us most. We have been seeking it, lo! these many years. We have set it up as an idol and worshipped it. We have loved peace more than we have loved honor, more than we have loved justice, more than we have loved truth, more than we have loved God; and we have lost it because we have loved it like that.

If a nation values anything more than religion, it will

lose its religion, and the irony of it is that, if it is comfort, or prosperity, or money, or peace that it values more, it will lose that too.

In the angels' song, peace is the middle term. The glory of God goes before it, and the good pleasure of God follows it. We shall find peace when we seek the glory of God. We shall know peace when we accept the will of God. "In His will is our peace."

You want peace. Ask yourself again what you mean by peace. Do you still mean freedom from fear, want, and oppression? That is not the peace of Bethlehem. Not for that did Christ come into the world.

This is Christmas time. Can we understand that Christmas is not a season but a spirit, that peace *did* come down from heaven to earth at Bethlehem – the peace of God's own presence? If we can understand these things, then perhaps, too, we shall understand why the little Prince of Peace is the only "Hope of the world."

This Christmas time we stand on the brink of the disaster of a divided world that has the hydrogen bomb in its bosom because it has not the spirit of Christmas in its heart.

We know what the bomb can do.

When will we recognize what *God* can do?

Bethlehem speaks to us of a new beginning, a new birth, a new life, a new hope. God says, "Behold, I make all things new," and only God can make things new. We can rearrange things, build on foundations already laid, use materials that are to hand. We can even improvise. Only God can recreate. Only He can bring about a new order in His old world.

The use of the H-bomb, and its near relations, the atomic bomb and nuclear weapons of various kinds, can only mean indescribable tragedy, catastrophic suffering, and diabolical destruction, if not the end of civilization altogether. Men everywhere know this, yet they cannot agree on a new order for the world in which these things would be outlawed. We have "The Parliament of Man," but not "The Federation of the World."

Our situation today is a challenge to us to let God bring in among us that new spirit of goodwill of which the angels sang; for certainly that is what we need – *and only God can give it.*

Upon us in this mighty Republic there rests a greater responsibility than upon any other people on earth, for this nation was founded "under God" by the faith of men and women who saw in His will the only way to freedom, justice, truth, and peace.

Every page of the gospel is aflame with condemnation of all that has brought the world to its present frightful condition.

"Violence is not an attribute of God," says the author of the Epistle to Diognetus, summing up the Christian philosophy of history. And has it not justified itself in experience? There could hardly be a better authority than Napoleon Bonaparte, who, after his mad career of crime and violence, said, "I have come to see that hardly anything can be achieved in this world by brute force alone." Thou hast conquered, O Galilean!

Has he?

Has He conquered in our minds? Have we come to see that ultimately there are only two alternatives: we can try to overcome evil with good, or we can try to cast out the devils by Beelzebub?

If we come to the place where this is a burning reality for us, then, with the Prince of Peace at our head as well as in our hearts, we can transform the terrible war potential of the world into a glorious co-operation of peoples seeking equal freedom, justice, and peace under God, who "made of one blood all the nations of men for to dwell on the face of the earth."

We can? No! *We* can't do it . . . but He can do it through us.

Come, then, let us hasten yonder;
Here let all, great and small,
Kneel in awe and wonder,
Love Him who with love is yearning;
Hail the star that from far
Bright with hope is burning.

—PAUL GERHARDT

Seven

The Word Became Flesh

Christianity sprang from an older religion, separated from it, and yet can never be understood properly apart from it. That religion was, of course, Judaism, the religion of the Jews, which is set forth authoritatively in the Old Testament.

It has sometimes been suggested that Christianity would do well to free itself entirely from the graveclothes of Jewry, and forget all about the Old Testament. I prefer to think of the Old Covenant not as the graveclothes, but as the swaddling bands of the New Covenant.

If we study the faith of the Old Testament in the light of comparative religion, we shall be compelled to believe that a special revelation was given to the Hebrews.

The exclusive nationalistic spirit of the Jewish people, which rebelled very strongly against foreign influences, the successful campaigns of the great Prophets against heathen practices and corruptions, the progressive development of an ever nobler faith, and, perhaps more than anything else, the desire for, and the belief in, a unique revelation to be given in "the last days" are sufficient evidence that we have here a distinctive and supernatural revelation.

People often wonder, Why did God choose the Jews? The tragic events of this century, bringing unparalleled sufferings to these ancient people, and involving all of us in a sense of shame and guilt, have raised the question in a new and vital way.

When we say that God "made man in his own image," we claim that God and man share, in some way, the same nature, so that fellowship between them is possible. We imply that God made man for fellowship with Himself.

If we had nothing more than this, it might be possible to maintain that God is concerned only with the relation of each individual soul to Himself. It *is* true that God is concerned with the relation of each individual soul to Himself. It is *not* true that this is His *only* concern.

The selection of a "Chosen People," and a particularly clannish nation, was necessary so that we may come to think of God not merely and only as related to individual souls, but also as related to a group, a "family," in which all the members are related to each other as well as to their common God.

But that is not all. He is "the Lord, the Creator of the ends of the earth." He is the God of all peoples and all nations.

In order for God to be fully revealed to all mankind, He chose a nation which, because of its special relation to Him, would be His agent in that world-wide revelation. Because God desires that all the nations of the earth shall come to a practical knowledge of Himself, *He chose the Jews to be His missionaries.*

If we consider this matter a little further, we shall come to see that not only the purpose of God but also the need of man calls for a revelation of this nature.

The Greeks had a different type of revelation – for we can call their intellectual attainments nothing less, but these were satisfying to the privileged few only. They left the hearts of the masses of the people as hungry as before, and the noble ideals of the Greek philosophers failed to raise the moral standards of that immoral country. Theories are not strong enough to influence the behavior of men while they remain theories. If God is going to reveal Himself in any satisfying manner, and with any adequate power, then that revelation must be embodied in a human character. That is why God chose the Jews.

His revelation to them was progressive. Each succeeding piece was greater as the mind of man evolved through experience and discipline to a higher stage of culture and intelligence. God lifted the veil fold by fold. First came the dispensation of Adam, then of Noah, then of Abraham, then of Moses, followed by the widening stream of the Prophets. One aspect of God's nature, one element in His purpose, reflected in the conditions of their time, the people could understand and accept. But God had to lead them step by step. The fullness of revealed truth in the beginning would have been unintelligible to them.

The Old Testament revelation came to different men in different ways. Samuel heard the voice of God like the voice of a man. Isaiah, Jeremiah, and Ezekiel had visions of God. Hosea learned of God's forgiving love through the heartbreaking experience of an unfaithful wife. The nation as a whole had to learn through bitter and repeated experiences of national calamity and captivity.

Each of the different messengers had his special emphasis. It was a revival of social justice in the fiery Amos, who vehemently denounced the existing social and economic sins of his people. In Isaiah it was a vision of the holiness of God, and a plea for undefiled monotheism. The Jonah, whom we so often regard as timid, made a lofty appeal for missionary enterprise.

These different types of revelation are plainly to be seen in the Old Testament. The diversity of the messengers, and of the content of their proclamations, speaks of the manifold love of God who revealed Himself in all the ways His children could understand, to prepare them for that great and glorious day when He should visit and redeem His people.

The whole history of Israel is a preparation for this perfect revelation of God. It is the voice of one crying in the wilderness, "Prepare ye the way of the Lord"; for whatever else God's coming may entail, it would be impossible without long previous preparation. It had to become the constant dream, the dominant expectation, and the central hope of a nation.

Judaism prepares for Christ because of its anticipation of a Saviour.

In spite of the amazing conviction of the reality of God and His providential care for His people which we find reflected in the Prophets, in spite of the approach to God which the sacrificial system of worship secured for every genuine seeker, in spite of the marvelous personal experiences of God recorded in the Psalms, the religion of the Old Testament is terribly conscious of man's need of a more convincing revelation of God, and throbs with the desire and hope that God would manifest *Himself* in an unmistakable manner. It is *God Himself* for whom the people long, and yet it is an ever more human figure that is being conceived as essential.

The more definite expression of this hope takes the form of the Messianic prophecies:

> *O thou that tellest good tidings to Zion, say unto the cities of Judah, Behold your God. He shall feed his flock like a shepherd.*
> *Behold a virgin shall conceive and bear a son, and shall call his name Immanuel.*
>
> *But thou, Bethlehem Ephratah, though thou be little among the thousands of Judah, yet out of thee shall he come forth unto me that is to be ruler in Israel; whose goings forth have been from of old, from everlasting.*

For unto us a child is born, unto us a son is given: and the government shall be upon his shoulder: and his name shall be called Wonderful, Counsellor, The mighty God, The everlasting Father, The Prince of Peace.

Here is woven together the idea of might and mercy, of law and love, of power and personality, in a fashion which can be understood *only* when, in the appearance of Jesus, we see what it is that the Prophets sought.

Israel's expectation had not only taken this personal form, but her history had been molded by mighty men who were dominated by the word of the Lord – the great Prophets of the Jewish people. At first a rather ecstatic utterance breaks forth from them; then we discover that although there is no searching of His understanding, they begin to appreciate the indwelling Spirit of God who controls their personality and reveals Himself in character rather than in speech. Finally, we see a Prophet like Hosea, whose life is a far greater message than anything he can actually say.

This spiritual development in one chosen nation is the preparation necessary for Christ's coming. But it was not the only preparation which was necessary, for while God chose the Jews to be His peculiar people, He did not forget the other nations of mankind, and among them, too, we can see His hand at work.

When Jesus was born, the whole of the then known world was welded into one empire, so that it is not too much to say that Caesar owned the world.

The great trade routes were trunk roads over which the couriers of Rome sped quickly. The seas had been rid of pirates and were safe for travel. Passports and travel documents were unnecessary. Greek was spoken and understood everywhere.

There was also an inward preparation of thought and feeling among the Gentiles. The culture of the ancient world prepared the way for Christ. Of course, it is true that "the world by its own wisdom knew not God," but the great philosophers and teachers were seekers after God, and some of their lofty ethical precepts would not be out of place in the New Testament itself. Greece, with its refined tastes and exquisite beauty, and Rome, with its farsighted laws and good general government, were steppingstones towards the truth as it is in Jesus.

Outside the boundaries of His own race there was, then, this twofold preparation for Christ's coming. Men everywhere were, in God's holy wisdom, being readied for "the fulness of the time."

It was into a world prepared both materially and spiritually for the Gospel to run swiftly without let or hindrance, into a world eager for good news of God, into a world straining after "something better," into a world anxious for an assurance of God's personal interest that Christ was born.

> *When the fulness of the time was come, God sent forth his Son, born of a woman, born under the law, that he might redeem them that were under the law; that we might receive the adoption of sons.*

* * * * * * * * * *

> *And the Word became flesh and dwelt among us, (and we beheld his glory, glory as of the only begotten of the Father), full of grace and truth.*

Here, in one of inspired Scripture's weightiest passages, St. John shows how the revelation – the "Incarnation" – of the Eternal Word realized and satisfied the dreams and yearnings of the children of men.

"The Word became flesh." This Creative Word, to whom everything owes its existence, who created us, Himself became a member of our humanity. He was God. He became flesh.

All Christian people believe that Christ now bears a

unique relation to God the Father. The New Testament tells us that He is "the Son of God," that "he sitteth at the right hand of God," that He is "in the bosom of the Father."

Such a relationship cannot have begun in time. Jesus could not have attained to it by virtue of the perfection of His earthly life. His moral character did not entitle Him to it. It was during the days of His flesh that He exercised God's prerogative of forgiveness, judgment, and redemption. These activities were not limited to those marvelous forty days of the post-resurrection appearances.

It was written of old, in the story of creation: "In the beginning God. . . ." Before the world was, ere time and its memorials began, God was. And even so it is written here, "In the beginning was the Word," timeless, even as God, without beginning, eternal. He was "with God" in the silence of eternity, and when that silence was broken by the symphony of creation, He was with God still – His Fellow Worker.

"The Word became flesh." The term "Word" need be no difficulty to anyone. What is an ordinary word? It is the means by which we express ourselves. Jesus is "the expression of God."

This first chapter of St. John's Gospel is the only passage in Scripture to ascribe the title "the Word" to Christ, but there is nothing said of Him here that is not implied either in His own teaching or in the Epistles. Our Lord Himself did claim to be the Messiah. Even in the Synoptic Gospels He exhibits a consciousness of a direct divine mission supremely important for His own race, and, before the close of His ministry, we can discover a growing conviction that the truth He was preaching was meant for a larger world.

Starting from and developing these ideas, His followers set themselves to express their own sense of their Master's unique religious value and importance, and some of them came up with thoughts which stagger the imagination to this day.

Who is the image of the invisible God, the firstborn of all the creation; for by him were all things created, that are in heaven, and that are in earth, visible and invisible, whether they be thrones, or dominions, or principalities, or powers; all things were created by him and for him, and he is before all things, and by him all things consist.

God, who at sundry times, and in divers manners, spake in time past unto the fathers in the prophets, hath, in these last days, spoken unto us in his Son, whom he hath appointed heir of all things, by whom also he made the worlds; who, being the effulgence of his glory, and the exact image of his person, when he had, by himself, purged our sins, sat down at the right hand of the majesty on high.

Let this mind be in you, which was also in Christ Jesus, who, being in the form of God, thought it not robbery to be equal with God, but made himself of no reputation, and took upon him the form of a servant, and was made in the likeness of men.

St. John's Gospel was written long after these quotations, and he injected a new element into the teaching of the Church when, in the opening verses, he referred to Jesus as "the Word."

Some scholars have suggested that the author of the Fourth Gospel borrowed this conception from the Alexandrian philosopher Philo. They trace its origin back to Egypt. I would trace it a lot further back.

In Philo, "the Word" is a vague and indefinite idea. It is most probably impersonal. It may be nothing more than his description of immanent reason. At all events, *it is very carefully distinguished from God.*

In this Gospel, the Word is personal. But more than that, *it is Divine* – "The Word was God." This divine, personal Being is active in creation, and voluntarily enters human life by becoming flesh, in order that, as the man Christ

Jesus, the historic Mediator, He may live among men and reveal the heart of God.

We have already seen that there is a similarity between the opening words of the Book of Genesis and the opening words of St. John's Gospel, and we do not need to look further for the Apostle's model, although we should remember that there are other passages in the Old Testament where the creation and government of the world, as well as the development of revelation, are traced to the Divine Word going forth from God as the active Agent of His holy will.

This "Word" of God, through whom God had been revealing Himself more and more fully throughout the ages, had, at last, actually become incarnate in the man Christ Jesus.

St. John sets this down as his sheet-anchor. That the Incarnation was an historical fact, that at some definite point in time the Eternal became material, the Everlasting became temporal, "the Word became flesh," is the heart of his message.

"The Word became flesh." The emphasis is not on the subject, "the Word," but on the predicate, "became flesh." As forcibly as possible St. John puts the contrast between the former and the latter conditions of Christ. "The Word *became flesh.*" He does not even say, "The Word became *man.*" He wishes both to emphasize the gulf crossed: *Word—flesh,* and to focus attention on *the reality of the manifestation.*

St. John was writing his *apologia* at a time when Christianity was being assailed by the deadly heresy which we call Gnosticism. Gnosticism was not content to deny the *reality* of the Incarnation, it denied the *possibility* of it as well. It taught that the flesh is the seat of evil and, as such, it could not possibly have been the vehicle of the Divine Word.

In the place of the Incarnation, the Gnostic teachers substituted a theory which said that the Good God — as distinct from the evil one who had created all matter — took pity upon men and sent Jesus Christ from heaven not as a man but as a "Saving Spirit" (*Spiritus Salutaris*), who assumed a phantasmal body which deceived the disciples into believing that it was a real body of flesh and blood.

It was St. John's aim to refute such a doctrine, and to state plainly, in terms which were familiar to his readers, that the Incarnation was an historical reality about which there could be no shadow of doubt. He set out to state a *fact* upon which his whole life and philosophy were based, the fact that in the man Christ Jesus God entered our humanity.

Our modern world is in need of this assurance. Perhaps there is no doctrine which we should emphasize more than this. People everywhere today are asking questions which the Incarnation answers. It is supremely relevent to every issue.

Deny the Incarnation and you deny the Gospel. "The Word became flesh, and dwelt among us." Either this is true, or Christianity is a hoax, a fraud, an imposition upon the credulity of men, a lie which should be exposed and destroyed.

"The Word became flesh, and dwelt among us." This is the basis for everything we believe about God. The essence of all our faith about Him is that once He was found in fashion as a man. This is the foundation of Christianity. What other foundation could we have?

* * * * * * * * * *

Previous to His incarnation, the Word knew the condition of men on earth — not only knew it, but regarded it with tender interest. The sad music of humanity entered His ear and touched His compassion. But it was the compassion of the Word, not of flesh.

It is one thing to look on suffering. It is another thing to suffer. It is one thing to watch a battle. It is another thing to fight. It was fitting that the Captain of our salvation should be made perfect through suffering.

Think for a moment of the pre-incarnate existence of Christ. Think of the glory, majesty, power, knowledge, and absolute perfection of the limitless God. Then think of flesh as symbolic of the human race — weak, limited, subject to weariness, hunger, trials, and sorrow.

Somehow, by some means, God took upon Himself our form.

It is not generally realized that although the Evangelist does not formally state the doctrine of the miraculous conception, yet he manages to imply it. He presents the entry of the Word into flesh as a creative act, just as the coming into being of the world was a creative act. He says nothing about the manner or process by which the Word became flesh, for the simple reason that He was not interested in it. St. John did not see the glory of God *about* Jesus, or *upon* Him, but *in* Him. A supernatural birth can be nothing more than the means for the entrance of the Divine. St. John goes further back, and presents the Divine which entered.

The Divine entered to make itself known. The Invisible became Visible. The Transcendent became Immanent.

God, the Eternal Other, is forever unknown and unknowable, except in so far as He willingly reveals Himself. "Canst thou by searching find out God?"

This does not mean, as many have erroneously taught, that God is totally unknown apart from Jesus, for as we know a man by his actions, so we may know God by and in nature. The material universe — the sun, the moon, the stars, the fields, the flowers, the sea, the wind — reveals its Creator in every twinkle of the stars, and every roar of the ocean.

The spacious firmament on high,
With all the blue ethereal sky,
And spangled heavens, a shinning frame,
Their great Original proclaim;

Th'unwearied sun, from day to day,
Does his Creator's powers display,
And publishes to every land
The work of an almighty hand.

—JOSEPH ADDISON

But it is a very partial and incomplete revelation. Indeed, Sir James Jeans, after studying the universe all his life, declares that the orderliness of nature convinces him that God is a mathematician!

The full and clear revelation of the living God cannot be confined to what we loosely call "dead matter." It tells us but a fraction about some of His attributes, though that knowledge is, of course, necessary and valuable.

Only when you have lived with a person, had intimate and constant fellowship with him, and seen his everyday life revealing the hidden secrets of his personality, can you really *know* him.

So the Word had to become flesh and dwell among us in order to reveal God fully and adequately. The purpose of Christ's coming was to make God known, and St. Paul tells us that in Him dwelt all the fullness of the Godhead bodily.

"The Word became flesh" to introduce into the human race a new life of sonship to the Father, and this new relationship Jesus first had to realize in His own Person, through all the stages of a complete human experience from birth to death.

His perfect obedience to the will of God in the lot appointed to Him – in His childhood, in the daily toil of the silent years in Nazareth, and in the exercise of His public ministry – was the indispensable foundation for His final sacrifice. He was the Second Adam, and where the first Adam failed, He succeeded. "For as through the one man's disobedience the many were made sinners, even so through the obedience of the one shall the many be made righteous."

Death came to Him in the fulfillment of His vocation.

It befell Him in His conflict with the world's evil. In the New Testament it is never spoken of as God's act. It is man's — "whom ye crucified." The Resurrection is God's act — "whom *God* raised up."

Jesus lived out His stainless human life as our Representative before the Father, and though, as a consequence, He was "by lawless hands crucified and slain," yet no man took His life from Him. He laid it down of Himself, because the work which He had freely undertaken included even this as a condition of its fulfillment.

But a dead Christ would have been no Christ at all. He rose again. Having become one with us in our condemnation, He had the right to make us one with Him in His triumph, to deliver us from the curse and bondage of sin, and to impart to us the glorious liberty of the children of God.

Light looked down and beheld darkness,
Thither will I go, said Light.
Peace looked down and beheld war,
Thither will I go, said Peace.
Love looked down and beheld hatred,
Thither will I go, said Love.
So came Light, and shone;
So came Peace, and gave rest;
So came Love, and brought life;
And the Word became flesh, and dwelt among us.
(*Source unknown*)

In the Word made flesh, God revealed His own Transcendent Personality before which our personalities may fitly bow down in the total self-surrender of adoration. That is why the Wise Men from the East journeyed to worship Him — they wanted to know what God was like. They found a Babe — but they fell down and worshipped Him. For those sages of old, the Child in the Manger had the value of God.

In the language of a famous New Testament scholar, "Jesus is the projection of God onto the screen of humanity." Eternity and time, the Divine and the human, are reconciled in this stupendous event.

Because He was perfect God, He was perfect Man – the Man God would have us be. Christ was not what we are, but what we should be.

The Stoics were amazing people. They portrayed a supposed "Ideal Man," and blithely said to their disciples, "Live up to that."

Jesus reveals the actual Ideal, and He says to us, "Let Me help you live like this," and we are thankful, for we know that it is impossible to be Christlike without Christ.

The Word did not become flesh to be our Friend, or our Companion merely. The Word became flesh to be our Saviour. To make Him anything less is to insult the Eternal Son of God who loved us, and gave Himself for us.

Somewhere, Dr. Henry Van Dyke tells the story of an agnostic philosopher who, one bleak winter, wanted to save the birds which visited his garden.

Pity filled his heart as he saw them feebly hopping over the frozen ground, looking for food, and scarcely able to move, so numbed were they by the cold. He opened his French windows and, laying a trail of food from the garden, tried to lure them inside the room, where warmth, food, water and shelter awaited them. But they would not enter.

He went outside and tried to drive them in, but he only frightened them out of his garden altogether. "Ah," said the agnostic, "if only I were a bird, they would understand, and would follow me, and I could save them."

And then, thinking further, the light flooded his being, and looking upwards he cried, "O God, now, at last, I understand. The only way You could save mankind was to become man Yourself, and through Your love for us, and Your oneness with us, lead us to safety."

"The Word became flesh, and dwelt among us."

The author wishes to express his thanks to Dr. Robert J. Cadigan, Editor-in-Chief of Presbyterian Life *magazine, for permission to reprint "Peace on Earth – What Does It Mean?", which appeared in the December* 8, 1956, *issue; "We, Too, Can Be Wise Men," which appeared in the issue dated December* 14, 1957; *and "God Made Us To Laugh," which appeared in the issue of December* 1, 1958. *These articles have been rewritten and expanded.*